The
PRAYING
WOMAN'S
~ *Devotional* ~

STORMIE
OMARTIAN

HARVEST HOUSE PUBLISHERS
EUGENE, OREGON

THE PRAYING WOMAN'S DEVOTIONAL
Copyright © 2008 by Stormie Omartian
Published by Harvest House Publishers
Eugene, Oregon 97402
www.harvesthousepublishers.com

ISBN 978-0-7369-6341-1 (pbk.)
ISBN 978-0-7369-6342-8 (eBook)

15 16 17 18 19 20 21 / VP-SK / 9 8 7 6 5 4 3

INTRODUCTION

I love reading the Word of God. I especially love it when the Scriptures I am reading inspire me to pray. And they always do. In this book I want to share with you certain verses I have chosen throughout the Bible, and how they have impressed my heart and mind and led me to pray specifically. I hope that as you read each one of these short Bible studies and devotional prayers, they will encourage you to see every verse of God's Word as a source of inspiration to draw you into a closer walk with the Lord through ongoing prayer.

I pray that each Scripture presented here will lead you to read it in your own Bible so you can reach further into the rest of that passage or chapter. There is much to be gleaned from reading Scripture in the context of its surrounding material when you have the time or inclination to do so.

In this book you will find examples of how to pray for your life and the lives of those around you, as well as for your world and the things you care about most. You will learn what God asks us to do with regard to prayer and how we should respond to His direction. You will be reminded of the ways God wants you to pray and why.

May each devotional and prayer encourage you to go deeper into God's Word to find the treasures God has for you there, and to pray in ways you might not otherwise have thought to pray. It is my prayer that each time you read in this book, it will bring inspiration for your day and hope for your future.

Stormie Omartian

God Always Hears You
When You Pray

*"Jesus looked up and said, 'Father, I thank you that you
have heard me. I knew that you always hear me, but I
said this for the benefit of the people standing here, that
they may believe that you sent me'" (John 11:41-42).*

Jesus showed up for a close friend's funeral—after he had already
been buried. He deliberately missed it all. When Lazarus became
sick, his sisters sent word to Jesus. But Jesus stayed where He was for
two more days, saying to His disciples, "This sickness will not end in
death" (11:4), and then, "Our friend Lazarus has fallen asleep; but
I am going there to wake him up" (11:11). They didn't understand
what He meant, so He finally told them, "Lazarus is dead" (11:14).

By the time Jesus arrived, Lazarus had been in the tomb for
four days. Mary and Martha found it hard not to express their
disappointment with Him. They knew He could have healed their
brother, but now they would have to wait until the resurrection to
see him again. In response Jesus said, "I am the resurrection and the
life. He who believes in me will live, even though he dies" (11:25).

When He arrived at the burial site, Jesus asked that the tomb be
opened. When the stone was rolled away, Jesus prayed, "Father, I
thank you that you have heard me." But this sounded like the *end*
of a prayer, not the beginning. Obviously, Jesus had been praying
all along. He had been talking to His Father for days as He always
did, but with full knowledge of this upcoming event.

It surely was difficult for Jesus to *not* be with His friends during
this tragic time. But He talked with God and waited for the right

moment so that God would be glorified in all that happened. He thanked His Father out loud for the benefit of all who were listening, and then He called Lazarus out of the tomb, grave clothes and all.

Jesus knew that His Father always heard Him. He knew days before that Lazarus would be resurrected. What a wonderful thing it is to be so certain that God always hears us when we pray. To trust completely that we are God's very own children and co-heirs with Christ (Romans 8:17).

God wants us to believe that He always listens to our prayers and will answer. He wants us to have an ongoing conversation with Him that keeps us in tune with His will and His purpose. He wants us to remember that Jesus brings life no matter how dead and helpless things seem. We just need to keep praying and believe in His ability and desire to answer.

*Father God, I thank You that I am Your child
and a joint heir with Christ. Because of that, I can
trust that You always hear my prayers. Help me to
maintain ongoing communication with You, just
as Jesus did, so that I may have a deep and abiding
walk with You and You will be glorified by my life.
In Jesus' name I pray.*

JESUS' PRAYER *for* YOU

*"My prayer is not for them alone. I pray also for
those who will believe in me through their message,
that all of them may be one, Father, just as you
are in me and I am in you" (John 17:20-21).*

Did you know that Jesus prayed for you and me? In this passage
Jesus was interceding for His followers, but He was also
speaking ultimately to every believer down through the ages.

We who have come to faith in Jesus can listen back in time to
this moment when the Lord prayed for *us*. We were on His mind as
He prepared to lay down His life in order to provide forgiveness for
our sins, abundant life now, and life with Him for eternity.

Jesus prayed for us to have unity with other believers—across the
nations, across cultures, across time, across the street, across the room,
across the sanctuary. He also prayed for us to have unity with Him
and the Father and the Holy Spirit so that our lives would convince
others of who He is. He declared His love for us and promised to
share His glory with us. He prayed for our salvation so that we could
be with Him forever, and He promised to continue to make Himself
known to us so we could experience more and more of His love.

Jesus was thinking of you centuries ago when He was praying.
He lives today and every day to "intercede" for you (Hebrews 7:25).
His desire is that you become one with Him and one with other
believers, so that those who see you will believe in Him. Pray that
you will always be one with Him and one with others. Thank Jesus
that even way back then, He was already praying for you.

*Father God, thank You that just as You and Your Son
are one, You want me to be in that kind of unity with
other believers. So I pray that no matter what church, race,
culture, denomination, city, state, or country Your children
are from, You will enable me to experience that same oneness
with them that Jesus prayed centuries ago for us to have.
In Jesus' name I pray.*

PRAYER GROWS LOVE
in YOUR HEART

 Read and Consider
2 Corinthians 9:6-15

*"And in their prayers for you their hearts will
go out to you, because of the surpassing grace
God has given you" (2 Corinthians 9:14).*

It is a powerful thing when we pray for one another. Every time we pray for someone, we feel more connected to them. It is exactly as Paul said—your heart goes out to the person you are praying for. That's because God gives us His heart for them.

That's why praying for our enemies is a good thing. It not only softens our heart, but it opens a door for them to hear God and for their heart to be changed. When there are people we are angry with and don't feel like praying for at all, if we will make ourselves pray for them, even though we don't feel they deserve it, walls will come down and forgiveness will happen.

Intercessory prayer is powerful on many levels. It not only influences situations and people, it changes *us* in the very process. Is there a difficult person for whom you need to pray? Has someone hurt you? Ask God to help you pray for them. When you do, He will work love in your heart for them, which will ultimately be to your greatest blessing. Only God can cause love to grow in your heart where there is none. Only God can bring to life love that has died. It happens as we pray for that person.

Lord, there are certain people I want to pray for, but it's very hard for me to do so. Yet I know You will give me Your heart of love for them when I do. Help me to pray especially for the people who have hurt me. Thank You that praying for others will not only affect their lives, but it will change my heart and life as well. In Jesus' name I pray.

GOD'S CONNECTION *with* Us

*"The LORD God formed the man from the dust of the
ground and breathed into his nostrils the breath of life,
and the man became a living being" (Genesis 2:7).*

God created the universe with a word. He spoke stars and
planets into existence. He formed the world with simple commands. God started the creation process without any preexisting
things. He began with nothing. With the presence of the Holy Spirit
and the entrance of His Word, creation happened. He brought order,
light, life, and beauty out of chaos and darkness. He said, "Let there
be…" and it happened.

Then He became personally involved with making humans. Other
places in Scripture describe God as a "potter" and human beings
as the "clay" (Isaiah 64:8), making us think of our heavenly Father
bent over a potter's wheel, forming mud figures into the design He
had in mind for us. The finishing touch was to breathe into us His
breath of life. God got personal, right from the start.

But He didn't stop there. God's action in giving us breath also
gave us the ability to speak. The act of breathing that keeps us alive
is the same act that we use to communicate. We breathe out to speak
(and some languages in the world even breathe in to speak). We are
God's image bearers (1:26-27). We breathe and speak because of
His breath given to us.

We should be in awe of the privilege we have to use the breath
of life to speak to our Creator. We were made to communicate with
our Maker. Even though we may not start out doing it very well, He
still wants to hear us speak to Him. Just as we are delighted when

our babies make their first tiny sounds, so our heavenly Father is delighted when He hears the sound of one of His children speaking words intended for His ears.

So breathe a prayer to God often. If words don't come to mind right away, start by saying, "Thank You." As you say those two words slowly, begin to add "for..." until different ways to end the sentence begin to flow. Once you do this a while, you will realize that you can use your inspiration (breathing in) as time to think of the next words and your expiration (breathing out) to express your gratitude. All the way back to the first breath of the first person, you and I were made for this. Giving us the "breath of life" is God's connection with us, and prayer is our connection with Him.

Lord, I thank You for the breath of life You have given me. I pray You will breathe new life into me today. Just as You spoke and brought about life in Your magnificent world, help me to speak words that bring life into my own small world as well. How grateful I am to be closely connected to You in every way. In Jesus' name I pray.

CRYING OUT *to* GOD

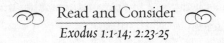### Exodus 1:1-14; 2:23-25

*"During that long period, the king of Egypt
died. The Israelites groaned in their slavery and
cried out, and their cry for help because of their
slavery went up to God" (Exodus 2:23).*

Have you ever felt like the Israelites in this passage? Perhaps
you too have endured a long season of repeatedly crying out
for deliverance. You might even now be in a difficult situation that
seems to offer no apparent means of escape. Perhaps you are hurting,
or someone you love is suffering, and you wonder if God can hear
your pleas for His help.

When the Israelites cried out, God not only heard them, He
answered them far beyond just helping them find relief. He totally
liberated them. But it happened God's way—the way that would
serve to teach both the Egyptians and the Israelites exactly who
He was. God raised up a leader in Moses—two leaders, actually,
because He also sent his brother, Aaron. Their first attempt to free
the people appeared to fail because the Egyptians ended up giving
Israel even more work than they had before. Even when Moses and
Aaron performed miracles, Pharaoh hardened his heart. The situation
looked more hopeless than ever. But in the midst of situations that
are dark and hopeless, God does His greatest work. Even though
the children of Israel were in bondage for nearly 400 years, "God
heard their groaning and he remembered his covenant...God looked
on the Israelites and was concerned about them." He will do the
same for you. When you cry out to God, your prayers will reach
His heart. Just remember that being set free from the past or from

a difficult situation may happen quickly or it can be a step-by-step process, depending on what God is wanting to teach you. You can't make it happen on your timetable, so be patient and continue to pray for as long as it takes. Don't ever stop believing that the Lord is a God of miracles.

Lord, I cry out to You for deliverance from anything that keeps me from becoming all You created me to be. Set me free from everything that separates me from You. Lord, I know that even in the midst of what seems to be the most hopeless situation, You can do Your greatest work. Thank You that You are a God of miracles. I pray You will do a miracle in my life today. In Jesus' name I pray.

GUIDANCE *for the* JOURNEY

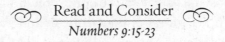

Read and Consider

Numbers 9:15-23

*"Whenever the cloud lifted from above the Tent, the
Israelites set out; wherever the cloud settled, the
Israelites encamped…At the LORD's command they
encamped, and at the LORD's command they set
out. They obeyed the LORD's order, in accordance with
his command through Moses" (Numbers 9:17,23).*

We all struggle on occasion with the weight of making a big decision. Should we take this job or that one? Say yes or no to our children when it comes to certain activities? Relocate our family to a different location or stay put? Wouldn't it be wonderful if we had a continual manifestation of God's presence to guide us like the cloud He provided for His children in the desert?

Despite this constant visual reminder of guidance, however, the Israelites still struggled with following and obeying. Learning to walk with God is a process. Just when we think we have it all figured out, God leads us into a new place where our old tricks won't work. In fact, we may feel as if we're learning to walk all over again. And in a way we are. We enter unfamiliar territory and are soon reminded that, on our own, we stumble. Yet when we take His hand, we walk with confidence. God wants us to soar far above the limitations of our circumstances and ourselves. He wants to take us to a place we have never been before and can't get to without His help. When God used Moses to lead the Israelites out of Egypt, they had to learn to depend on the Lord for every step of their journey to the promised land. When they did not do that, they got into trouble. It's the same for us today.

If you are at a place in your life where you feel as if you can't take one step without the Lord's help, be glad. He has you where He wants you. If you're wondering, *Have I done something wrong?* the answer is most likely that you've done something right. God has you on this path, regardless of how difficult and impossible it may seem right now, because you are willing to follow Him. He wants to accomplish great things through you that can only come out of a life of faith. He wants your undivided attention because you can't do these things on your own. The path is not a punishment; it's a privilege. It's not a restriction; it's a reward.

Lord, guide me on my journey through life. Help me to understand and recognize Your leading in every decision I make. Give me clear direction so that I can stay on the path You have for me. I know following You doesn't mean everything will be easy. Help me to not lose faith when the road gets rough. I want to always arrive at the place You want me to be In Jesus' name I pray.

GOD IS NEAR WHEN WE PRAY

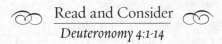

Read and Consider
Deuteronomy 4:1-14

"What other nation is so great as to have their gods
near them the way the LORD our God is near us
whenever we pray to him?" (Deuteronomy 4:7).

It is comforting to know that whenever we pray to our God, He
is present with us. The truths that Moses was teaching to the
Israelites still hold true for believers today. Our God is alive, He is
close, He is responsive. The Lord is here to listen and to bring wisdom,
insight, and transformation into hopeless situations. He is here to
protect and guide His people on the paths He desires them to walk.

Moses reassured the Israelites about their privileged status as the
people of God. He reminded them that they were not like the people
of foreign lands whose gods could not respond to them. Their God
would remain with them at all times and would hear their prayers
whenever they called on Him.

What does this mean for us? Does it mean that God isn't close to
us unless we are praying? No. He is always with us, just as His presence traveled constantly with the Israelites to guide them. However,
when we pray, we are drawn into a deeper awareness of His presence
and a clearer understanding of His nature. Prayer reminds us of who
we are in relationship to Him. Prayer puts us in a place where we
can hear from Him and be changed by Him. No amount of prayer
to a lifeless idol could ever accomplish that. We pray to a living and
responsive God who loves us and wants to be an active part of our
lives. When we don't pray, we miss out on the benefits of a close
walk with Him. Draw near to Him in prayer right now and sense
His presence in and around you.

*Lord, I thank You for being close to me when I pray.
Thank You that You hear and will answer me. Thank
You that in Your presence there is transformation for my
soul and my life. I draw close to You now and ask for
an ever-increasing sense of Your presence. I ask that You
would help me to pray more and more every day and
give me increasing faith to believe for the answers.
In Jesus' name I pray.*

GIVE *the* GIFT *of* PRAYER

"As for me, far be it from me that I should sin against the LORD by failing to pray for you. And I will teach you the way that is good and right" (1 Samuel 12:23).

You might not think of a failure to pray for others as a sin against God, but Samuel clearly considered it so. God calls us to support one another, love one another, and pray for one another. When we don't do these acts, we are not living in the unity and fellowship that He desires us to have, and we cannot experience all the blessings that He wants to give us. Samuel knew this and proclaimed that he would be faithful in prayer for the Israelites—in spite of all of the evil they had done in God's eyes.

Prayer is the greatest gift we can give to anyone. Of course, if someone needs food, clothes, and a place to live, those needs must be met too. But in giving that way, we also should not neglect to pray for that person as well. Material things are temporary, but our prayers for another person can affect him or her for a lifetime.

We can never move into all God has for us until we first move into intercessory prayer. This is one part of our calling that all Christians have in common because we are *all* called to intercede for others. God wants us to love others enough to lay down our lives for them in prayer.

Lord, I pray for each member of my family and for all of my friends and acquaintances to be blessed with peace, good

*health, provision, and a greater knowledge of You and Your
Word. Help me to know how to pray for each person. Show
me if I have forgotten anyone. May I never sin against You
by failing to pray for other people according to Your will.
In Jesus' name I pray.*

Overflowing *with* Joy, Peace, *and* Hope

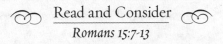

Read and Consider

Romans 15:7-13

"May the God of hope fill you with all joy and peace as you trust in him, so that you may overflow with hope by the power of the Holy Spirit" (Romans 15:13).

We live in a culture that is busy with activities and offers more options than we could ever have time for. We sometimes run on empty more than full, much less overflowing. Yet Paul's prayer for the believers in Rome was that their souls would be so full of joy, peace, and trust that they would overflow with hope. This was to happen not by their own strength or the sheer force of their wills, but "by the power of the Holy Spirit."

Would you like to overflow with hope? Would you like to be a person whose joy seems to light up every room, whose peace can be felt in even the tensest situations? Then by the power of the Holy Spirit, praise God! It's no accident that in this passage Paul quotes from Old Testament passages about praising God, singing hymns to His name, and rejoicing! That's how we find hope in God. Through praise and worship. When we connect to God and honor His presence in our lives, and when we praise Him for His character and the evidences of His works in us, we have so much of Him in us that He spills over. God's gifts in us become our gifts to those around us. That's when we overflow with the joy, peace, and hope that come only from God.

*Dear God, help me to avoid the things that would
deplete my soul or minimize my strength. Fill me
instead with Your hope, peace, and joy, so much so
that they overflow from me to others. I praise You for
who You are and thank You that as I do, Your Holy
Spirit pours new life into me. Fill me afresh with Your
Spirit today and take all weakness and worry away.
In Jesus' name I pray.*

OPEN MY EYES, LORD

∾ Read and Consider ∾
2 Kings 6:8-23

*"And Elisha prayed, 'O LORD, open his eyes so he may
see.' Then the LORD opened the servant's eyes, and he
looked and saw the hills full of horses and chariots
of fire all around Elisha. As the enemy came down
toward him, Elisha prayed to the LORD, 'Strike
these people with blindness.' So he struck them with
blindness, as Elisha had asked" (2 Kings 6:17-18).*

Elisha and his servant were surrounded by an enemy army, but
Elisha knew something his servant didn't, so he prayed that
God would open his servant's eyes—*really* open them. When God
did just that, the servant saw an even greater army of God surrounding the whole scene.

Elisha's prayer is one we can all pray too. "Open my eyes, Lord.
Help me to see the *real* picture, the big picture, the supernatural
picture. Help me to see what You are doing. Lift the curtain off of
my spiritual eyes so that I can see Your hand at work behind the
scenes of the battles I face in life."

But there is another prayer in this story. After Elisha prayed that
his servant would see the truth of God's supernatural protection, he
then prayed that his enemies would be struck blind so they couldn't
see what was around them. This would cause them to follow a different path. Both of Elisha's prayers were answered. There are times
when we also need to pray Elisha's second prayer. We need to ask
God to blind and confuse our enemy.

Ask God to give you the ability to see with spiritual eyes so you
can better understand things from *His* perspective.

*Almighty God, I pray You would open my eyes to see the
truth about my situation. Give me clear understanding—
especially when I am facing the enemy—of all You
are doing in the midst of my situation. Help me to
trust Your hand of protection. Enable me to see things
from Your perspective so that I can stand strong.
In Jesus' name I pray.*

CALL *on the* NAME *of the* LORD

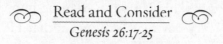
"Isaac built an altar there and called on the name
of the LORD. *There he pitched his tent, and there*
his servants dug a well" (Genesis 26:25).

Isaac was having a difficult time. It seems that everywhere he turned he got into trouble. Abimelech got after him for lying; the Philistines stopped up his wells in order to force him to move away; and even after he moved and dug a new well, someone argued with him about *that* one. He couldn't win.

With each situation, however, he avoided conflict and worked for peace for everyone involved. Finally, when it seemed that everything was peaceful, the Lord appeared, describing Himself as the God of Isaac's father, Abraham. "Do not be afraid, for I am with you; I will bless you and will increase the number of your descendants for the sake of my servant Abraham" (26:24).

This surely must have caused Isaac to flash back to the many times when his dear father had talked about the Lord. What had Abraham taught him? What did Isaac feel about this God who had stopped his father's knife and sent a ram instead as a sacrifice? Did he have memories of being untied and taken back home—and how joyful his dad had looked on that return trip? This God was not to be taken lightly. This God introduced Himself to Isaac, giving him a wonderful promise of future blessing. Isaac acknowledged that promise and "called on the name of the Lord."

What does it mean to call on the name of the Lord? It means to acknowledge who He is and the power of His very existence to do more than we can ask or think. It means to place our trust in Him and praise Him for all He does. When you call on the Lord's name, you give Him the praise that He deserves by recognizing Him in all of His holiness, authority, and glory. In doing so, you open yourself to the power and blessing He wants to bring into your life.

Praise God every day for all the ways that He is sufficient for every need you have, and, like Isaac, declare your faithfulness to Him by calling on His name in prayer.

Lord, You are the God of the universe and Lord of my
life. I worship You and give glory to Your name. You are
holy and wonderful—amazing and awesome—and I
thank You for all You have done for me. Because Your
Word says You are able to do beyond what I can even
think of to ask for, I call on You to meet all of my needs
in ways more wonderful than I can even imagine.
In Jesus' name I pray.

Pray *for* Godly Friends

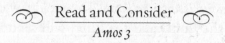
*"Do two walk together unless they have
agreed to do so?" (Amos 3:3).*

So much is made of the importance of the right kind of friends
in the Bible that we can't treat this part of our lives lightly.

The main quality to look for in a close friend is how much that
person loves and fears God. What Amos wrote is a picture of being
in agreement on many levels. You will have all different kinds
of friends, but your closest friends—those with whom you walk
closely—should be the kind of friends who impart something of the
goodness of the Lord to you every time you are with them.

Following are signs of a desirable friend:

A desirable friend tells you the truth in love. "Wounds from a friend
can be trusted, but an enemy multiplies kisses" (Proverbs 27:6).

A desirable friend gives you sound advice. "Perfume and incense
bring joy to the heart, and the pleasantness of one's friend springs
from his earnest counsel" (Proverbs 27:9).

A desirable friend refines you. "As iron sharpens iron, so one man
sharpens another" (Proverbs 27:17).

A desirable friend helps you grow in wisdom. "He who walks with
the wise grows wise, but a companion of fools suffers harm" (Proverbs
13:20).

A desirable friend stays close to you. "A man of many companions
may come to ruin, but there is a friend who sticks closer than a
brother" (Proverbs 18:24).

A desirable friend loves you and stands by you. "A friend loves at all
times, and a brother is born for adversity" (Proverbs 17:17).

A desirable friend helps in time of trouble. "Two are better than one, because they have a good return for their work: If one falls down, his friend can help him up!" (Ecclesiastes 4:9-10).

A desirable friend is not rebellious. "Do not join with the rebellious, for those two [the LORD and the king] will send sudden destruction upon them, and who knows what calamities they can bring?" (Proverbs 24:21-22).

A desirable friend is not often angry. "Do not make friends with a hot-tempered man, do not associate with one easily angered, or you may learn his ways and get yourself ensnared" (Proverbs 22:24-25).

Pray that God will give you good, godly friends who will influence and encourage you to grow deeper in Him.

*Lord, I pray I would always have good, godly friends, and
that we would influence, encourage, and inspire each
other to walk closer to You. I pray for friends who will
tell me the truth in love, give me sound counsel, and be
a help in times of trouble. Enable me to be that kind
of friend too. Send desirable friends into my life.
In Jesus' name I pray.*

Jesus Teaches Us How *to* Pray

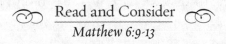

Read and Consider

Matthew 6:9-13

"This, then, is how you should pray: 'Our Father in heaven, hallowed be your name, your kingdom come, your will be done on earth as it is in heaven. Give us today our daily bread. Forgive us our debts, as we also have forgiven our debtors. And lead us not into temptation, but deliver us from the evil one'" (Matthew 6:9-13).

Few people can enter a church without hearing this prayer either spoken or sung. It's known around the world. In Jerusalem there is a building that has over one hundred beautiful ceramic tiles inscribed with the words of this prayer in many languages of the world. Some people call it the "Our Father" or the "Lord's Prayer." Whatever title you use, it's accurate to say that this is probably the best known and most repeated prayer in the Christian world.

It is called the Lord's Prayer because Jesus, our Lord, taught His disciples to pray in this manner. He did not intend for them to mindlessly repeat this prayer over and over. Rather, He was laying out a pattern of prayer for them, and for us today as His disciples, to follow. There is rich meaning in each phrase.

Our Father in heaven, hallowed be your name is a declaration of praise acknowledging that God is holy and to be revered. His name is never to be taken lightly. Not only is He Lord of heaven and earth, but He is also our heavenly Father.

Your kingdom come, your will be done on earth as it is in heaven reminds us that God wants us to pray for His will to rule and reign in our world. As we pray and invite God to manifest His power in the midst of earth's suffering and pain, He will move in response to our prayers. His power and presence will enter our lives and will work out on earth what He has willed in heaven.

Give us today our daily bread declares our dependence upon God as our provider. All that we have now has been provided by His gracious hand. Everything we need in the future will come from Him day by day as we seek Him for it.

Forgive us our debts, as we also have forgiven our debtors is a statement in which we not only ask God for forgiveness, but we are also reminded that we must forgive others. Just as we are indebted to God because He forgave our sins, so we must willingly forgive those who have sinned against us.

Lead us not into temptation, but deliver us from the evil one. Jesus was not saying that God tempts people but that we have an enemy of our souls who would like nothing better than to defeat us. We all go through times of temptation from which we need divine deliverance. But Jesus paid an enormous price so we could be free and have power over the evil one.

Some manuscripts include: *For yours is the kingdom and the power and the glory forever. Amen.* All that God is and all that God does lives forever. There has never been and never will be anything greater than God in all the universe. This declaration reminds us of that.

Heavenly Father, I praise Your holy name. I pray You will reign in my life and rule in this world. Pour out Your Spirit on this land so that Your people may do Your will. I depend on Your provision, forgiveness, and protection from the enemy. I praise You for all You are and all You do. In Jesus' name I pray.

LOOKING *for* GOD'S WILL

*"Do not let this Book of the Law depart from your
mouth; meditate on it day and night, so that you may
be careful to do everything written in it. Then you
will be prosperous and successful" (Joshua 1:8).*

Who doesn't want to know God's will for their life? And God wants to reveal it. So why does God's will often seem to be such a mystery to us? In order to know what God wants, you need to be aware of four important aspects of His will:

First, God's will is most often found through reading the Bible and letting it sink into your heart. Joshua was commanded to know the Book of the Law backward and forward, to meditate and reflect on it. Then God promised to prosper him. The Bible declares clearly that God will direct and lead us. Psalm 37:23 says, "If the LORD delights in a man's way, he makes his steps firm." And in Psalm 32:8, God promises, "I will instruct you and teach you in the way you should go; I will counsel you and watch over you." He speaks to us through His Word, the Scriptures.

Second, God's will is ongoing in our lives. From the time we are infants until the day we die, God has a will for us—as children, young people, adults, and senior citizens. Isaiah 58:11 says, "The LORD will guide you always; he will satisfy your needs in a sunscorched land and will strengthen your frame. You will be like a well-watered garden, like a spring whose waters never fail."

Third, God's will is specific. The prophet Isaiah heard the Lord promising His children, "Whether you turn to the right or to the left, your ears will hear a voice behind you, saying, 'This is the way; walk in it'" (Isaiah 30:21).

Fourth, God's will is profitable. The Lord told Joshua, who was to lead the Israelites into the promised land, "Do not let this Book of the Law depart from your mouth...be careful to do everything written in it. *Then you will be prosperous and successful*" (Joshua 1:8, emphasis added).

Looking for God's will may be simpler than you ever imagined. It doesn't matter what your situation is at the moment. As you read the Word and prayerfully ask for guidance, then all you have to do is take the next step that the Lord is showing you. As you take one step at a time, you will begin to see a solid way of following after God. As long as you are walking with Him continually in prayer and living His way according to His Word, you are not likely to get off the path of His will. And if by chance you do, He will get you right back on. That's because when you're always listening for God's voice, you will sense in your heart when you violate His directions. Each small step of obedience will turn into a life of obedience lived in the will of God.

Dear Lord, I pray that every time I read Your Word, You will teach me what I need to understand. Help me to comprehend Your truth. Speak to me specifically about how each passage I have read relates to my life and to the lives of others. Enable me to meditate deeply on Your Word and take steps of obedience in response to it so that I can live in Your perfect will and prosper as You have promised. In Jesus' name I pray.

Your Heavenly Father Waits *to* Hear *from* You

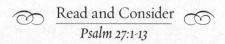 Read and Consider
Psalm 27:1-13

"Though my father and mother forsake me, the
LORD will receive me" (Psalm 27:10).

When Jesus' disciples asked Him to teach them to pray, He gave them a model beginning with the words "Our Father" (Matthew 6:9-13). Some of us have no problem thinking of God as a Father. We had good dads, or at least adequate ones, and the imagery of God in relationship to us as our Father is a positive one.

For others of us, however, thinking of God as a Father is troublesome, if not downright painful. Perhaps you're in that category. Your earthly father may have abandoned you or neglected you or even abused you. How do you wrap your mind around the concept of a heavenly Father when you have conflicted feelings about the earthly father who failed you in that category?

God says that in order to have a long, fruitful life and move into all He has for you, you must honor your father and mother (Exodus 20:12). It's a command! You may have had parents who were around and provided food and a place to live—and for that you certainly need to be grateful—but maybe they never put anything of themselves into your life. Maybe you could never expect Dad or Mom to support, encourage, or teach you anything.

But you still need to honor them, if for no other reason than that they gave you life. Without them, you wouldn't be here. But you can't fully honor your father and mother if you haven't forgiven them. No parent is perfect. No parent always does everything right. Ask God to show you if there is anything you need to forgive. Even if your parents are no longer living, forgiving them will clear the way for you to fully see God as your heavenly Father and to feel His love for you. He will heal and restore whatever you suffered or lost in your relationship with your parents.

Praise God that He is the perfect Father—loving, kind, accessible, helpful, encouraging, guiding, and comforting. Regardless of what your earthly father was like, your heavenly Father will be everything you need. Look to Him every day.

Dear Heavenly Father, I thank You that You will never forsake or desert me. Thank You that You always accept me. I am grateful for Your love, guidance, and comfort. Show me any place in my heart where I have not forgiven my own father or mother for anything they may have done or not done. I want to honor You by honoring them with complete forgiveness. In Jesus' name I pray.

GOD DOES MORE THAN YOU CAN IMAGINE

⮎ Read and Consider ⮌
1 Chronicles 17:1-27

*"And now, LORD, let the promise you have made
concerning your servant and his house be established
forever. Do as you promised, so that it will be established
and that your name will be great forever. Then men
will say, 'The LORD Almighty, the God over Israel, is
Israel's God!' And the house of your servant David will
be established before you" (1 Chronicles 17:23-24).*

More than anything, David desired to build a magnificent temple to honor the Lord. He had big plans and all kinds of resources ready. Even Nathan the prophet thought a temple was a great idea. Then God spoke. Through a revelation to Nathan, God revealed that David would not be the one to achieve that goal. The message Nathan shared began with God's "no" but ended with amazing promises to David. One of David's offspring (Solomon) would indeed build the temple, and David's throne would be established forever.

Rather than complaining about being denied the temple project, David responded with deep humility, gratitude, and praise. God was giving more than he ever dreamed—a temple and an everlasting kingdom! David acknowledged that this great blessing had to do with God's character and grace, not David's own worthiness (17:16-19). He praised God saying, "There is no one like you, O LORD" (17:20). He described the parallel between God's gracious choice of his family and God's faithfulness to Israel, both examples of God's amazing willingness to work out His plans through frail and flawed people. Then David made a request: "Let the promise you have made…be established forever" (17:23). In today's language, David was praying, "Lord, these are the amazing promises You have made about my family. I know that because You have said it, it will be done!"

Whenever you sense that God is saying no to your prayer, don't focus on your disappointment over not having *your* will done. If you do that, you may miss the joy of something much better that can come about if *God's* will is done. God's will is always richer and better than anything you can imagine.

Lord, I confess any disappointment I have had when my prayers were not answered the way I wanted them to be. I know my greatest blessing will come about because of Your will being done in my life. I also know that what You have for me is far greater than what I can imagine for myself. Forgive me for any time I did not trust that to be true. In Jesus' name I pray.

Ask, Seek, *and* Knock

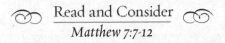

Read and Consider
Matthew 7:7-12

"Ask and it will be given to you; seek and you will find;
knock and the door will be opened to you. For everyone
who asks receives; he who seeks finds; and to him who
knocks, the door will be opened" (Matthew 7:7-8).

If Jesus instructs us to ask, seek, and knock, why do we sometimes struggle to pray as much as we should? One reason could be that we doubt God will really hear and answer. Or we fear being disappointed if we ask for too much or for the wrong thing. Or our own self-sufficiency may keep us from total dependency upon God. Or perhaps we feel that if God knows what we need before we ask, why do we need to ask?

Yet Jesus Himself, who knew the heart of Father God better than anyone, teaches us that we must be diligent to tell God our needs and pursue Him by faith. "Without faith it is impossible to please God, because anyone who comes to him must believe that he exists and that he rewards those who earnestly seek him" (Hebrews 11:6).

Often we feel reluctant to bring our needs to God because we think our problems are too big, or too small, or our own fault—therefore, we can't bother God about them. But the good news is that we are God's beloved children, and He is our loving Father. We can feel free to ask Him for the desires of our heart and that they be in alignment with His will. "Seek his kingdom, and these things will be given to you as well" (Luke 12:31).

Jesus' promise is that if we imperfect parents desire to give good gifts to our children, "how much more will your Father in heaven give good gifts to those who ask him!" (Matthew 7:11). So don't hesitate to ask, seek, and knock, knowing that your heavenly Father hears and will answer.

*Lord, I come to You in faith, believing You are
God, and that You reward those who diligently seek
You. Your Word says You desire to give good gifts to
those who ask for them. I ask that the desires of my
heart be aligned with Your will so that they will
come to pass. I knock on the door of opportunity for
my life, and anticipate it being opened by You.
In Jesus' name I pray.*

GOD WILL GET YOU THROUGH

*"Should you then seek great things for yourself? Seek
them not. For I will bring disaster on all people,
declares the LORD, but wherever you go I will let
you escape with your life" (Jeremiah 45:5).*

Jeremiah's scribe, Baruch, surely suffered as much as Jeremiah.
After he recorded everything Jeremiah heard from the Lord, he
read the prophecies publicly. Then he had to read them again before
a group of leaders, after which he was instructed to go into hiding
with Jeremiah. A little later he heard his scroll had been sliced to
pieces and burned. To his surprise (and probably terror), Jeremiah
gave Baruch another scroll and said, "God has told me to do it over.
Let's start." Baruch became discouraged and afraid, but he also
prayed. And God answered.

God gave Jeremiah a special message for Baruch. He told Baruch
he would preserve his life in all circumstances. God warned him to
not seek great things for himself because *everyone* would experience
adversity. But God promised to rescue *him*.

The assurance of God's presence must have been a powerful
comfort to Baruch. That same assurance is available to us. God has
said, "Never will I leave you; never will I forsake you" (Hebrews
13:5). Jesus promised, "I am with you always, to the very end of the
age" (Matthew 28:20).

These promises do not mean that nothing bad will ever happen
to us. They mean that we can count on God's presence as we face
all that life brings our way. Even in the midst of terrible circumstances, God is with us, saving us in ways we may not even be able to

comprehend at the time. Jesus said, "I have told you these things, so that in me you may have peace. In this world you will have trouble. But take heart! I have overcome the world" (John 16:33).

It doesn't matter what your circumstances are at this moment, God has a future for you that is filled with good things. Even though you may have to go through tough times, take God's hand and walk with Him. He promises He won't let you fall.

Lord, I pray You will be with me in the most difficult and trying times of my life, helping me in ways I may not even be able to comprehend. I know that even though there may be troubles ahead, when I walk with You, You won't let me fall. When I go through difficult situations, help me not to complain, for I know You will make a way through or provide a means of escape.
In Jesus' name I pray.

GOD SEES OUR
HEART TOWARD HIM

≋ Read and Consider ≋
1 Samuel 14:24-45

*"Then Saul built an altar to the LORD; it was the
first time he had done this" (1 Samuel 14:35).*

What is your relationship with God *really* like?

That question needs to be answered because some people *appear* to have it all together spiritually. They serve in the church and do all the right things, but they don't have a true personal and life-giving relationship with Jesus.

Take Saul, for example. Handsome and strong. King of Israel. Chosen by God. Yet the Bible records here that Saul made an oath to not eat until he avenged himself on his enemies. This may have looked God-honoring, but it was unwise and impulsive and left his army stranded without sustenance. Later, he built an altar to God, but this was the first time Saul had done this—the first time the king of God's people had done the most basic act of honoring God!

The next chapter takes us even deeper, for it tells how Saul imploded as a leader, becoming completely unable to follow God's explicit instructions. In the end, Samuel tells Saul: "Does the LORD delight in burnt offerings and sacrifices as much as in obeying the voice of the LORD? To obey is better than sacrifice, and to heed is better than the fat of rams" (1 Samuel 15:22).

We don't want to be the kind of people who love God with our words only. We don't want to obey Him just because we have to or because our church says we have to. We want to have hearts so full of love for God that we can't contain it. We want to obey God because we can't bear the thought of disappointing Him. We don't want to be the kind of people who pray only when things are rough. We want to eagerly anticipate time with God each day because we love Him and enjoy His presence. God knows the difference.

Always remember that God's love for you is far beyond what you can even imagine. Ask Him to fill your heart with that kind of love for Him in return.

Dear God, help me to have such a big heart of love for You and Your ways that is always pleasing in Your sight. I don't want to be a person who shows love for You with only words. I want to show it with my actions, my obedience to Your laws, and the way I live my life. Thank You that You love me at all times—even when I don't do everything right. In Jesus' name I pray.

Thank God That He Knows *and* Loves You

Psalm 139:1-24

*"O LORD, you have searched me and you know me. You
know when I sit and when I rise; you perceive my thoughts
from afar. You discern my going out and my lying down;
you are familiar with all my ways" (Psalm 139:1-3).*

God knows everything about you. He knows your thoughts even
before you think them. "Before a word is on my tongue you
know it completely, O LORD" (139:4). He knows your actions from
the time you rise in the morning until the moment you go to bed
at night. Even when sleep reduces you to unconsciousness, He is
watching over you still.

God is everywhere around you. There is nowhere you can go that
God is not there too. He is with you in the mountaintop experiences
of life, and He is with you in the valleys of despair. He is omnipresent.
Corrie ten Boom suffered in a Nazi prison camp during World War
II yet was able to write, "There is no pit so deep that God is not
deeper still."

God did a miracle in creating you! You may struggle with the way
you feel or how you look, and you may not feel much like a "miracle"
at all, but you are. You may feel more like a mistake, but you are
not. God formed you and loved you even when you were in your
mother's womb. You bear His image (Genesis 1:27).

Your life is no accident, and the purpose of your life was ordained
even before you were born. Your heavenly Father knows everything
about you, is present everywhere around you, and performed a

miracle when He made you. Praise God every day that He knows you and loves you!

Dear God, I thank You that You know everything about me and You still love me. You know my thoughts and my mistakes, and You still call me Yours. Thank You that You are always with me—teaching and guiding me, comforting and restoring me—and I am never alone. You, Lord, know me better than I know myself. Help me to know You better too.
In Jesus' name I pray.

The POWER of LITTLE by LITTLE

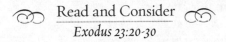

Read and Consider

Exodus 23:20-30

*"Little by little I will drive them out before
you, until you have increased enough to take
possession of the land" (Exodus 23:30).*

Have you ever asked God to do something major in your life,
and then experienced disappointment when He appeared to
be working little by little rather than all at once?

Perhaps you have a lifestyle habit that you know is unhealthy.
You've asked God to remove those persistent physical urges, but you
grow discouraged when the progress you're making seems insignificant. Or maybe, like the Israelites, you are coming under attack
from adversaries who seem intent on your personal or professional
destruction. Why doesn't God, who certainly has the power, give
us victory instantaneously or wipe out the enemies that cause so
much harm?

There are no simple answers, but this passage provides an important clue about the nature of God's activity on our behalf: He is
going by His timetable, not ours, and His will for us is determined
by what is ultimately best for us. Scripture tells us that "with the
Lord a day is like a thousand years, and a thousand years are like a
day. The Lord is not slow in keeping his promise, as some understand
slowness. He is patient with you" (2 Peter 3:8-9). Our loving heavenly
Father is working for our eternal good, but He is accomplishing
His purpose in our lives in His own perfect way and in His own
time. God knows that these little steps are better for us now. He
doesn't want us to be overtaken by the things that could happen if
we experience victory too quickly.

Be encouraged when your prayers reveal progress that can be measured even in the tiniest increments. God is at work in your life and in the lives of those around you, and before long, little by little will add up to major change.

God, help me to have the patience to wait on You for the answers to my prayers. I confess I want all the answers to manifest now, but I know Your timing is perfect. Help me to understand the things that are happening in response to my prayers that I cannot see. Enable me to see the step-by-step progress that is being made, and to trust You when I don't see any at all. In Jesus' name I pray.

CHANGING *the* WORLD
with OUR PRAYERS

∽ Read and Consider ∽
Acts 13:1-3

*"While they were worshiping the Lord and fasting, the
Holy Spirit said, 'Set apart for me Barnabas and Saul
for the work to which I have called them'" (Acts 13:2).*

At a prayer meeting in the early church at Antioch, the Lord set
forth a plan that changed the world (Acts 13:1-3). Members of
that congregation recognized that change would involve two things:
their response to the Holy Spirit that brought them to prayer and
fasting, and their sending forth Barnabas and Saul in ministry.

And the world *was* changed. It is an observable fact that history
turned on the basis of that prayer meeting in Antioch, Syria, nearly
two thousand years ago. Any historical analysis shows that the flow
of events that has shaped the world as we know it today—notably
Western civilization—can be directly traced to that prayer meeting.

People who pray and understand who they have been made to
be in Christ set the direction of history in their world—be it local,
regional, national, or international. Most of the believing church
today thinks of faith in Jesus Christ as an escape. But God says
He wants us to be instruments of redemption through intercessory
prayer, and ministry will flow out of that.

That's why it is so important to have prayer times with other
believers. In fact, *it is impossible to grow and develop to your fullest
potential independently of other believers.* It can't be "just me and
God all the way." We have a mutual dependence upon one another
because we are defined and refined within the context of a local body
of believers. *Building a people to do God's work happens in the local*

church when we are connected to and grow with the rest of the body of Christ. It is within that context that we find who we are created to be and what we are created to do.

One of the most important things about being in a spiritual family is finding power in prayer through unity. When believers are in unity, there is a dynamic that adds power to our prayers and the confidence that God will answer in power. Believers praying together can change the world.

Lord, I know my calling and purpose is revealed in prayer. I know it is defined within a church body of believers with whom I can grow. Help me to be in the church body You want me to be in so that I can pray with others in unity and power and be refined by Your Spirit. Enable me to understand and be set apart for the work You have for me to do.
In Jesus' name I pray.

KNOWING GOD IS *with* YOU

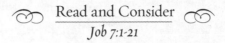 Read and Consider
Job 7:1-21

*"What is man that you make so much of him, that
you give him so much attention?" (Job 7:17).*

Job was at the end of his rope. He was suffering greatly, with no
understanding of why. His question came out of his frustration. In
essence, he was saying, "We're worthless, God, so stop paying attention to us humans! Maybe then we'd be left in peace. Maybe then
we wouldn't be tested and examined and constantly found wanting."

Job knew he wasn't a hypocrite. He knew he'd lived a life pleasing
to God. In his pain he lashed out at God. But his friends con-
cluded that he must have committed some horrible sin in order to
deserve such unbearable punishment. Surely they understood that
all people suffer—yet the extent of Job's suffering seemed to need
an explanation.

When we are careful to obey God's rules and directions for our
lives and repent when we sin, we may feel as if we should be exempt
from suffering. After all, why would God allow faithful people to
endure such hardships? But God uses difficulties, pain, suffering, and
trials to make us stronger, wiser, and more able to comfort others.

God is the Lord, the Savior of our souls, the Lover of our hearts.
He isn't sitting up in heaven watching us in our misery. He is with
us every step of the way, working His perfect will in our lives.

God says, "As the heavens are higher than the earth, so are my
ways higher than your ways and my thoughts than your thoughts"
(Isaiah 55:9). You may not understand your suffering, just as you
cannot understand the depth of God's love for you. But keep open
the lines of communication between you and Him. If you feel angry

because of your situation, tell Him. He understands. As you praise Him for who He is, He will heal your heart and bring good out of the situation.

Heavenly Father, it is hard to comprehend the depth
of Your love for me and why You care about the details
of my life. I am grateful that in difficult times You are
with me, walking beside me all the way through to the
other side of pain and trouble. Where bad things have
happened and I have blamed You, I ask for Your forgiveness.
Thank You for always working things out for my good.
In Jesus' name I pray.

The POWER *of* GOD'S PROMISE

 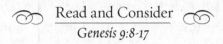
*"Whenever the rainbow appears in the clouds, I will see it
and remember the everlasting covenant between God and
all living creatures of every kind on the earth" (Genesis 9:16).*

When the clouds part after a thundershower revealing a stunning arc of colors, how many times have you stopped to look—and even called to others to join you? "Look at the rainbow!" Never ceasing to be objects of wonder, rainbows are those amazing creations that disappear as quickly as they appear, yet bring joy to our hearts when they surprise us by parting the gray with their luminescence.

That arc of color ties us right back to our ancestor Noah, to the moment after the flood when God made a promise, a covenant, that He would never again destroy the earth with a flood. Many scholars believe that the people of Noah's day had never even seen rain—that instead, the earth had been watered from springs deep in the ground. The flood occurred when "the springs of the great deep burst forth, and the floodgates of the heavens were opened" (7:11). Rain fell from heaven—and would continue to fall for the rest of the ages. But Noah did not need to fear the next time rain clouds gathered because God had made a promise. The rain would subside and the rainbow would appear. That visual sign would be a constant reminder that God always keeps His promises.

What does that have to do with prayer? Everything! When we pray, we reassert our faith that God keeps His promises. What we say out loud, or silently in our hearts, proclaims the truth of God's promises that we have read or heard in His Word. Have you ever noticed that if you are feeling bad and you keep saying negative thoughts out loud, you tend to feel them even stronger? The same is true in believing God's promises. When we speak the truth about God and about what He has promised us, while refusing to believe the lies of the enemy, it causes us to believe God stronger than before. That is not to say we should deny we have real problems or struggles, but the way we interpret them may be different. Satan wants us to believe that God has abandoned us and reneged on His promises, but God wants us to know that His promises are always true in spite of what we can see from our limited human perspective. By asserting our belief in His promises in prayer, we put ourselves in a position to see a lot more from God's perspective and a lot less from the enemy's.

So the next time you stand in wonder at the appearance of a rainbow in the clouds, breathe a prayer of thanks to God that He will always keep His promises.

Lord, I thank You that You always keep Your promises
to me. Help me to understand and remember exactly
what Your promises are so that I can recall them in my
mind, keep them in my heart, and speak them out loud
whenever I need to push doubt away from me. Help
me to remember that Jesus is the ultimate proof that
You have already kept Your greatest promise to us.
In Jesus' name I pray.

STANDING BEFORE OUR HOLY GOD

∽ Read and Consider ∽
Isaiah 6:1-8

*"'Woe to me!' I cried. 'I am ruined! For I am a
man of unclean lips, and I live among a people
of unclean lips, and my eyes have seen the
King, the LORD Almighty'" (Isaiah 6:5).*

When Isaiah, one of God's greatest prophets, had a vision of God with the angels worshiping Him around His throne, he realized his own unworthiness and sin. He said, "I am ruined!" When he confessed his sin, God touched him and purified him. God's holiness made him aware of his own lack of it. It also made him whole.

Sin chips away pieces of our soul. With enough sin, we become a pile of broken pieces. But God's holiness is what purifies us and helps us to separate ourselves from all that is *unholy*. There is a correlation between God's holiness and our wholeness. That's why when we are in His presence, we become more whole. *God's holiness makes us whole.* Whenever the great men of faith in the Bible, such as Job, Abraham, and Moses, had a close encounter with God, they saw their own failings. That's what happens to us too.

You may be thinking, *Why do I need to become more aware of my own failings? I am already well aware of them. Thinking about them is just going to make me feel worse about myself than I already do.*

But understanding God's holiness doesn't make you feel bad about yourself in a way that leads to depression. It makes you feel drawn toward His holiness in a way that leads to restoration. It convicts you rather than condemns you. It's actually liberating.

The Bible tells us to "approach the throne of grace with confidence, so that we may receive mercy and find grace to help us in our time of need" (Hebrews 4:16). We certainly should be humble as we bring our unworthiness to His throne. Yet we can be confident because we know we are called and loved. We can come to God anytime, knowing that He wants us there and that He will cleanse our hearts and make us more like Him.

Ask the Lord to help you comprehend His holiness. Then acknowledge your own lack of it and pray that who He is will rub off on you.

Dear Lord, whenever I sense Your holy presence, I am greatly aware of my own unworthiness. And that makes me even more grateful for how much You have done for me so that I can come before Your throne with confidence and find Your mercy and grace in my time of need. Touch me and purify me and help me to separate myself from all that is unholy.
In Jesus' name I pray.

CRYING OUT *for* GOD'S MERCY

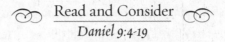 Read and Consider
Daniel 9:4-19

"Now, our God, hear the prayers and petitions of your servant...We do not make requests of you because we are righteous, but because of your great mercy" (Daniel 9:17-18).

Daniel had many reasons to be deeply alarmed. His own people were in exile, and he was pleading with God for the end of their captivity and their return to Jerusalem. But Daniel wasn't asking God for His help because the people deserved it. He was making his request because he knew God was a merciful God. Daniel cried out, "but because of your great mercy." Daniel was begging God to extend compassion and mercy to the people because of who *the Lord* was, not because of who the people were. His passionate prayer was a petition to a holy and righteous God—a God who grants grace in difficult situations because of His nature. Grace is not something that we can ever earn or deserve. Even our very salvation is a work of God's grace. "For it is by grace you have been saved, through faith—and this not from yourselves, it is the gift of God—not by works, so that no one can boast" (Ephesians 2:8-9).

When we are going through difficult circumstances, we can ask God's help even though we don't deserve it. Just like the tax collector Jesus described in one of His parables, we can say, "God, have mercy on me, a sinner" (Luke 18:13). Then praise Him that His help isn't dependent on what we do or on our "works," but on who *He* is.

Dear God, I come to You, not because I am worthy, but because You are. You are full of mercy, and I need Your

mercy extended to me today. I need Your help with all
things, but especially with certain situations in my life right
now. I thank You that Your help isn't dependent upon my
good works, but upon Your goodness, love, and grace.
In Jesus' name I pray.

Deliverance May Be
Only *a* Prayer Away

∽ Read and Consider ∽
2 Chronicles 18:28-34

"When the chariot commanders saw Jehoshaphat, they
thought, 'This is the king of Israel.' So they turned to attack
him, but Jehoshaphat cried out, and the LORD helped him.
God drew them away from him" (2 Chronicles 18:31).

The kingdom of Israel had divided into two kingdoms, Israel and Judah. While these kingdoms were often at odds, they did join together to fight Aram. Judah's king, Jehoshaphat, was known for being a righteous king, but this was not a trait that could be used to describe Israel's wicked King Ahab. Even though the prophet Micaiah had foreseen doom for Israel and the death of Ahab, the two nations had a common enemy in Aram, so it seemed to make political sense to go into battle together.

As a precaution against the prophecy of his own death, King Ahab shrewdly suggested that he remain in disguise as a soldier, while Jehoshaphat enter the battle in a king's full regalia. Even those of us who've never entered a battlefield would know that the enemy army is going to want to take out the leader. If the king is leading his army, he is the primary target. But Jehoshaphat agreed. And sure enough, when the enemy attacked, they went after the only king they saw. But Jehosphaphat prayed, and God protected him. And in keeping with the prophecy, a stray arrow found the chink in Ahab's armor even though he was disguised as a mere soldier.

Jehoshaphat made several errors that day, not the least of which was building an alliance with a competing and wicked king. He asked for a prophet of God but didn't really listen when he came.

He let his faith slip in the face of political expediency, pride, or even fear. But one choice Jehoshaphat made was impeccable. Even in the heat of battle, he cried out to God.

Prayer is not something that only happens in the quietness of a moment. Acknowledging God's presence and power—talking to God—should be part of every aspect of life, the battles as well as the peace times. Always cry out to God in your desperate moments, remembering that deliverance is often only a prayer away.

Lord, I pray You would strengthen my faith so that I will not give up praying in the heat of the battle of opposition from the enemy. I pray You will bring total deliverance to me from any strongholds the enemy may be trying to erect in my life right now. Enable me to stand strong in prayer, praise, and worship, giving thanks for Your presence and delivering power on my behalf. In Jesus' name I pray.

Nothing Is Impossible *with* God

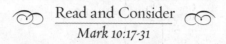

Read and Consider
Mark 10:17-31

*"Jesus looked at them and said, 'With man this
is impossible, but not with God; all things
are possible with God'" (Mark 10:27).*

The most exciting thing about God being all-powerful is that it means *with God, all things are possible.* There is nothing too hard for Him. Gabriel told Mary that "nothing is impossible with God," and look what happened to her (Luke 1:37). Jesus said, "All things are possible with God," and look what He accomplished! There is nothing that God cannot do. God's power is not limited.

If you have ever lived through an earthquake, tornado, or hurricane, you know that their power is overwhelming and frightening. Yet God has absolute power over all those things. May I suggest that we don't really *want* to experience the *full* magnitude of God's power?

Suffice it to say that God has far more power than is necessary to meet your needs and lift you above your situation. He has more than enough power to rescue you from your circumstances and help you do things you could not do without Him. If God is so powerful that He can create something from nothing or give life to the dead, then think what He can do in your life. He has the power to do whatever is necessary, and He doesn't want you to doubt it.

*Dear God, You are all-powerful and nothing is too hard for
You, not even changing the most difficult circumstances of*

*my life. What is impossible for me is not impossible for You,
so I ask that You would do the impossible and transform
me into a holy person full of Your love, peace, and joy.
Enable me to do great things by the power of Your Spirit.
In Jesus' name I pray.*

WHEN GOD SAYS NO

*"Go and tell my servant David, 'This is what the LORD says:
Are you the one to build me a house to dwell in?…When
your days are over and you rest with your fathers, I will raise
up your offspring to succeed you, who will come from your
own body, and I will establish his kingdom. He is the one
who will build a house for my Name, and I will establish
the throne of his kingdom forever'"* (2 Samuel 7:5,12-13).

S ometimes, God says no.
　　None of us like to hear no for an answer. We don't want to
be told no when we ask for help, or no when we ask someone for
something, or no when we want to buy something new. We want
to hear yes, yes, yes!

David fully expected a yes from God—and so did Nathan the
prophet. After all, David wanted to honor God greatly by building
a majestic place of worship. What could be wrong with that? In
fact, Nathan was so certain of God's yes that he told David to go
ahead and follow his heart. It seemed to him like a good plan with
good motivation.

Then God stepped in. "That night the word of the LORD came
to Nathan" (7:4). And Nathan realized he had to tell King David
that even though the plan seemed good, it wasn't *God's* plan.

When God says no, it doesn't mean He doesn't care for us. In fact,
quite the opposite. It means He has a greater purpose, and He knows
the outcome. What you asked for might be dangerous, or unwise, or
second-best. Or what you asked for may be wrong—perhaps your
motivation or attitude was wrong. God wisely says no. So when you
hear a no from God, trust His wisdom. It may even be signaling

a *yes* in another direction! David received a disappointing no from God, but he also saw a future yes. David's son, Solomon, would build the temple with more glorious resources at his disposal than anyone ever before him.

When God says no to some of your prayer requests, thank Him for His wisdom and revelation, and tell Him you look forward to the good that He will send your way instead.

Dear Lord, I trust You and accept Your answers to my prayers, even when the answer is not what I want. Help me to always understand Your will, especially when Your answers to my prayers are not what I expected or thought they would be. I am grateful that You know what is best for me and will not allow me to seek after things I shouldn't.
In Jesus' name I pray.

PRAYER *and* THANKSGIVING BRING PEACE

"Do not be anxious about anything, but in everything,
by prayer and petition, with thanksgiving, present
your requests to God. And the peace of God, which
transcends all understanding, will guard your hearts
and your minds in Christ Jesus" (Philippians 4:6-7).

These familiar verses remind us to pray and bring all our requests to God so that we can have His peace ruling our hearts. But what we often forget are the two words, "with thanksgiving." We neglect to thank God in the midst of whatever is happening (or *not* happening) to us at the time. We don't remember to praise Him first as the source of all that we will ever need. We don't always remember to worship Him for who He is. And we must do that, because all the things that are true of God are true of Him no matter what is going on inside of us or in our lives.

Just before this verse, Paul tells all of us to rejoice in God. He even says it twice for emphasis. We are instructed to "rejoice in the Lord always" (4:4), to find our joy in Him. So many times we think our fear and anxiety are connected to God. We think we feel that way because of something He didn't do or may not do for us. *What if He doesn't provide for us? What if He doesn't protect us? What if He doesn't give us what we want or need?* But what if we, instead, were to say in the face of these feared problems, "Thank You, Lord, that You will always provide for us." Or, "Thank You, Lord, that You are my protector and You will continue to protect me." Or, "Thank

You, Lord, that You have promised to give us everything we need and give us the desires of our hearts."

Anxiety can come into our souls at any time. It often happens in the middle of the night when the house is quiet but the mind is not. There are pills that promise temporary relief, but when they wear off, the anxiety is still there. The problem has simply been masked. Such anxiety can only be quieted by the peace of God. And the moment we receive Jesus, we have access to peace that "transcends all understanding." When we are fearful, apprehensive, worried, or terrified, the peace of God can restore us to calm, assured confidence.

We have access to that peace every time we praise God and give Him thanks. It's best to do it the moment we sense anxiety over *anything*. And then *continue* to praise and thank Him until all anxiety leaves. Try it and you'll experience greater peace than you have ever known.

Dear God, help me to not be anxious or worried
about anything. Help me to pray about all that
concerns me instead. Enable me to lift up praise and
worship in the face of all that opposes me. Enable me
to bring every concern before You and leave it at Your
feet. Teach me to refuse to think what-if thoughts. Fill
me with Your peace that passes all understanding
so that my heart and mind will be protected.
In Jesus' name I pray.

The BENEFITS of WAITING on GOD

*"Blessed is the man who listens to me, watching daily at
my doors, waiting at my doorway" (Proverbs 8:34).*

When you are sitting at a stoplight, standing in a long checkout
line at the supermarket, or flipping idly through an old
magazine in a physician's waiting room, do you ever think, "What
a blessing it is to wait"?

If you're like most people, you probably hate to wait. We are
busy people; we usually have more to do in any given day than we
can possibly accomplish. And yet over and over again, Scripture
speaks of the need for us to wait—and *commands* us to do so. "Be
still before the LORD and wait patiently for him" (Psalm 37:7). The
key is waiting for *Him.*

The Bible teaches that waiting for *Him* is actually a blessing in
our lives.

This verse tells us that we are blessed when we listen to God and
watch and wait daily at His doors. But how does God use times of
waiting to bless us?

When God permits life's circumstances to delay us from our
intended goal, we can be sure He has good reason. It might be to
build our faith because the New Testament teaches that "faith is
being sure of what we hope for and certain of what we do not see"
(Hebrews 11:1). When we are forced to wait, our faith must become
stronger.

Or God might use times of waiting to build our character as we
wait for the character of Christ to be formed in us. "And we, who
with unveiled faces all reflect the Lord's glory, are being transformed

into his likeness with ever-increasing glory, which comes from the Lord, who is the Spirit" (2 Corinthians 3:18).

Or God may be wanting us to wait so that we can learn to be patient. As we wait with hopeful anticipation for Him to work in our situation, He has promised that we will be "strengthened with all power according to his glorious might so that you may have great endurance and patience, and joyfully giving thanks to the Father" (Colossians 1:11-12).

God loves us, so our times of waiting on Him must be ultimately beneficial to our emotional and spiritual growth. The next time you are tempted to become restless during a time of waiting on God, use that time instead to praise God for all the benefits and blessings that He has in store for you. And don't forget to thank Him that His timing is perfect.

Lord, help me to wait on You and listen for Your
voice speaking to my heart about the things I need
to hear. Teach me all I need to know. Thank You
for the great blessings that await anyone who waits
at Your feet and listens for Your direction. In these
times of waiting on You, may the character of Christ
be formed in me and my faith be ever increasing.
In Jesus' name I pray.

ASKING GOD *for* WISDOM

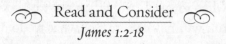
"If any of you lacks wisdom, he should ask God,
who gives generously to all without finding fault,
and it will be given to him" (James 1:5).

If every time we pray for wisdom God will generously give it to us, then we should be praying for wisdom every day and not just when the need is urgent.

The most urgent time that we pray for wisdom is when we are in a difficult and pressing situation and we don't know what to do. We need help. We need to know which way to go. And we usually need to know immediately. In those times it's comforting to know that God is not only available to us and willing to help, but He has *promised* to do so.

However, we don't have to wait until we are in an emergency situation in order to pray for wisdom. We can pray now. How many times have we faced a quick decision or an immediate situation in which our response would have been a lot stronger, better, or more effective if we'd had more of God's wisdom beforehand? King Solomon, when invited to make any request he wanted to God, asked for wisdom early in his reign. And God gladly granted his request (1 Kings 3:5-10). We need to do that too. In other words, we should ask *before* the need arises.

If you don't have God's wisdom, you will try to get through life on your own strength and understanding, and you may end up making bad decisions or doing stupid things. But when you ask God to give you wisdom every day, you will find yourself doing things so wise even *you* may be surprised. You will make a decision that turns out to be so completely right that you will be amazed. You will have insight you never had before. You will be able to give sound advice to someone who asks for it. You will sense danger when it is lurking. You will know when to speak and when not to, and what to say and how to say it. You will have a sense of what to do and what not to do in any situation.

Ask God for wisdom right now. You can trust that He will give it to you because He has promised it in His Word.

*Dear Lord, I ask for wisdom, for I know true wisdom
comes only from You. Thank You that Your Word
promises You will give wisdom to me when I ask for
it. Help me to be wise every day in every decision,
especially when I must act quickly. Enable me to know
what to do and what not to do in any situation.
In Jesus' name I pray.*

WHEN WE FACE DECISIONS
and DIFFICULTIES

∽ Read and Consider ∽

Acts 14:21-28

*"Paul and Barnabas appointed elders for them in each
church and, with prayer and fasting, committed them to
the Lord, in whom they had put their trust" (Acts 14:23).*

Whenever God said something important to His people, or
whenever an important decision had to be made, prayer,
often accompanied by fasting, preceded it.

When the apostles had to choose a replacement for Judas, they
gathered all the believers and "joined together constantly in prayer"
Acts (1:14).

When the believers in the church in Jerusalem began to face
severe persecution, they prayed for boldness, raising "their voices
together in prayer" (4:24).

When it became apparent to the Christians who had converted
from Judaism that even Samaritans could be saved, they sent Peter
and John to pray for these new followers of Jesus (8:15).

When Saul (Paul) had been struck blind, he fasted and prayed
for three days, waiting to see what God would do (9:9).

When God wanted to send His message beyond the borders
of Jerusalem, Judea, and Samaria and to "the ends of the earth"
(1:8), He sent His message to Peter as he was praying (10:9) and to
Cornelius as he was praying (10:30).

When Peter was imprisoned, the church gathered to pray for
him (12:12).

God set apart Saul (Paul) and Barnabas while the church at
Antioch was worshiping and fasting (13:2).

It comes as no surprise then, that when Paul and Barnabas had to help organize the leadership in the churches they planted, they did so only after prayer and fasting (14:23). They couldn't stay in each church; they had to move on. For a church to continue to thrive, solid Spirit-filled leaders were needed. So Paul and Barnabas sought the Lord and waited for His guidance. As a result the churches grew even after Paul and Barnabas left.

When we face big decisions, difficult circumstances, or hard questions, we should always turn to God first and pray. When we combine prayer with fasting, our prayers gain new power. We are trusting God and only God to be our nourishment and fill our hunger with His Spirit. It is especially powerful when we do that in unity with other believers. So when seeking the Lord's guidance, whether for issues regarding your personal needs, or for the needs of others in your family, community, nation, or world, don't take a step without seeking God in prayer first.

Lord God, I know when I fast and pray my prayers
gain new power. Help me to do that whenever I have
to make important decisions and I must have Your
guidance. Enable me to have the discipline to fast
regularly so that I can be prepared when I have to
make quick decisions. Make me ready to handle
the great opportunities You have ahead for me.
In Jesus' name I pray.

Just Enough Light for the Step You're On

*"'In accordance with your great love, forgive the sin of
these people, just as you have pardoned them from the
time they left Egypt until now.' The LORD replied, 'I have
forgiven them, as you asked'" (Numbers 14:19-20).*

The history of the Israelites in the desert was checkered with times
of eager obedience and great joy along with times of stubborn
disobedience and great punishment. God had performed many
miracles to deliver His people from Egypt, yet they still continued
to doubt Him. He then took them into the desert and tested them.

One test involved water: He let them go without it for three
days. God knew the people needed water, and He could easily have
provided it for them. But they didn't ask. They didn't pray. They
complained. And that was part of the test. God wanted them to ask.
He wanted them to be dependent on Him for everything. When
Moses cried out to God on their behalf, God said that if the people
would listen to Him and do what He commanded, He would meet
all their needs. So they listened and obeyed. They got their water
and were content.

Until the next crisis.

Instead of learning something from the water situation, the
Israelites complained again about their lack of food. God was not
trying to starve them. He knew they needed food, and He wanted
to provide it for them. But He wanted them to come to Him and
rely on Him for it. Once more, Moses prayed and God provided.
But this time, God provided only what was needed for each day,

one day at a time. God desired that they trust Him for each day's provision. He wanted them to learn to walk with just enough light for the step they were on.

Does this sound at all familiar? Can you think of anyone you know who wants to get to the "promised land" but doesn't want to do what's necessary to make the trip? Are you aware of a person who desires to have everything he or she needs but is not willing to give up anything to get it? Have you ever felt that you should have already arrived, without having to trust God for every step to get there?

This passage illustrates that God's capacity for forgiving the sin and foolishness of His people is unlimited. We need only confess, and He is faithful and just to forgive us (1 John 1:9). At the same time, results follow our rebellious behavior. God will forgive us, but sometimes we have to experience the consequences of our sin. In this case, the people would eventually die in the desert, and of those then alive, only Joshua and Caleb would ever see the promised land.

God often provides just enough light for the step we're on, but we have to trust Him and walk in obedience to His leading. Then He will illuminate the next step we are to take.

Dear God, just as You walked with Your people in the
desert after You delivered them out of Egypt, and You
forgave them and provided what they needed every
step of the way, I turn to You for deliverance and
forgiveness and ask that You would provide for my
needs every day. Help me to never doubt that You will
always give me the light I need for each step I take.
In Jesus' name I pray.

Finding Deliverance

"For Zion's sake I will not keep silent, for Jerusalem's sake I will not remain quiet, till her righteousness shines out like the dawn, her salvation like a blazing torch" (Isaiah 62:1).

Isaiah interceded for the deliverance and restoration of his nation with fervency and desperation. Yet he also prayed with the hope of a man who had a vision for the future of his people.

We need to pray with that same combination of desperation and vision. Once we recognize that our only hope for deliverance and restoration in our lives is found in God, it causes us to pray with passion. Yet we are hopeful because we know that nothing is impossible with God. We know that in His hands, anything is possible. In His hands the situation will be resolved, the question answered, the wound mended, the oppression dissipated.

Isaiah's prayer reminds us of several things. First, it reminds us of the passion we must have in prayer not only for our own lives, but also for the lives of others in our family, our city, and our nation. Next, it reminds us that our only hope is in God, even if we fool ourselves into believing for a time that we can take care of things ourselves. Finally, Isaiah's prayer reminds us that no matter how hopeless the situation seems, God is our hope. We are never in a dark situation with no light. He is our light, and we just have to open our eyes and see Him.

All lasting deliverance comes from the Lord, and it is an ongoing process. It is God who has "delivered us from such a deadly peril, and he will deliver us. On him we have set our hope that he will continue to deliver us" (2 Corinthians 1:10). God does a complete work, and He will see it through to the end. So don't give up because it's taking longer than you hoped. Be confident that "he who began a good work in you will carry it on to completion until the day of Christ Jesus" (Philippians 1:6).

No matter how difficult your situation seems, don't give up because God will not rest until your righteousness shines out like the dawn and your salvation like a blazing torch (Isaiah 62:1).

Lord, I know my only hope for total liberty and restoration in my life is found in You. You have saved me for all eternity and for Your glory, and nothing is impossible with You. So I thank You that You will not give up on me until I am completely set free from anything that keeps me from becoming all You created me to be. Thank You that You are restoring me to complete wholeness, and my righteousness will shine forth like the morning sun. In Jesus' name I pray.

PRAYING *for* YOUR CHILDREN

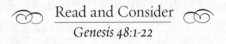
"Then he blessed Joseph and said, 'May the God before whom my fathers Abraham and Isaac walked, the God who has been my shepherd all my life to this day, the Angel who has delivered me from all harm—may he bless these boys. May they be called by my name and the names of my fathers Abraham and Isaac, and may they increase greatly upon the earth'"(Genesis 48:15-16).

If you are a parent (or a grandparent), God has given you the authority to pray for your children. You know your children better than anyone else. You know their hopes, their fears, their secret worries, their insecurities, their dreams, their gifts, and their abilities. You love them more than life itself. No one has a heart for their well-being and their future more than you do.

God has not only entrusted you to care for your children's physical, emotional, and spiritual needs, but He has given you a way to bless them as well. Through prayer. The most important thing you can do as a parent is bring your children daily before the Lord and pray for His protection, guidance, wisdom, and love to be infused into every part of their lives. And even though you can't always be with your children every moment, God can. And you can trust that He will be with them in power when you pray.

Each time you intercede for your children, pray that God will bless their lives and give them wisdom and discernment in the choices they face. Pray that He will protect them from the traps the enemy sets for them and that they will follow God and reject evil. Pray that they will love learning and discover the gifts and abilities that God has given them. And pray that their lives will bring glory to God and hope and healing to those around them.

Prayer is the most important gift you can give to your children. They will thrive under the care and power of a praying parent.

Heavenly Father, help me to pray daily for my children and grandchildren and any other children You put in my life. Bless each child with a knowledge of who You are and help them to live Your way so they can stay on the path You have for their lives. Enable each child to recognize the gifts and talents You have put in them, and to follow Your leading as they develop and use them for Your glory. In Jesus' name I pray.

The LORD IS NEAR WHEN WE PRAY

Read and Consider
Psalm 145:1-21

"The LORD *is near to all who call on him, to all*
who call on him in truth" (Psalm 145:18).

Do you experience times when God seems far away? Most of us do. The psalmist speaks for us when he cries out, "Why, O LORD, do you stand far off? Why do you hide yourself in times of trouble?" (10:1). When He was hanging on the cross, Jesus cried out, "My God, my God, why have you forsaken me?" (Matthew 27:46).

Our feelings may tell us that God is distant, but Scripture tells us otherwise. When we call on Him in prayer, God is near to us whether we *feel* it or not. At the same time, we might pray for something we need and fail to see an answer after weeks, months, or even years of passionate intercession. Why does God so often cause us to wait for what we are so sure we need right away?

We may be denied certain things for a time because God wants us to fervently pray and intercede for them. He wants to do something great in response to our prayers, something that can only be birthed in prayer. There may be things that won't happen in your life unless you are praying long and fervently about them.

If you start becoming discouraged and feel as if your life won't ever be any different than it is at this moment, know that the truth is quite the opposite. It's at these very times, when you feel as though you're not getting anywhere or you're missing the future God has for you, that God is actually *preparing* you for your future. And when the time is right, He has been known to do a very quick work. Draw close to God in prayer, trusting that He is near. Thank Him that He hears your prayers and will answer in His perfect way.

Lord, I draw close to You and thank You that You are
close to me. I confess the times when I have doubted
You were near to hear my prayers, because it seemed
my prayers went unanswered. Now I know that doubt
is contradictory to Your Word. Help me to pray even
more fervently during times of unanswered prayer
instead of being concerned that nothing will change.
In Jesus' name I pray.

LEARNING *to* LISTEN

*"Therefore, this is what the LORD God Almighty, the
God of Israel, says: 'Listen!'" (Jeremiah 35:17).*

This is not a complicated direction God is giving His people. It can't get any simpler than, "Listen!" He said it then, and He's still saying it today. God wants us to listen to Him only. That's why we have to be discerning about what we allow into our minds.

We have a choice about what we will accept into our minds and what we won't. We can choose to "take captive every thought to make it obedient to Christ" (2 Corinthians 10:5), or we can allow the devil to feed us lies and manipulate our lives. Every sin begins as a thought in the mind. "For from within, out of men's hearts, come evil thoughts, sexual immorality, theft, murder, adultery, greed, malice, deceit, lewdness, envy, slander, arrogance and folly" (Mark 7:21-22). If we don't take control of our minds, the devil will.

That's why you must be diligent to monitor what you allow into your mind. What TV shows, magazines, and books do you look at? What music, radio programs, or CDs do you listen to? Do they fill your mind with godly thoughts and feed your spirit so you feel enriched, clear-minded, peaceful, and blessed, or do they deplete you and leave you feeling empty, confused, anxious, and fearful? "God is not a God of disorder but of peace" (1 Corinthians 14:33). When we fill our minds with God's Word and godly books and magazines written by people in whom God's Spirit resides, and we listen to music that praises and glorifies Him, we leave no room for the enemy's propaganda.

Refusing to entertain unrighteousness in your thought life is part of resisting the devil. If you want to determine whether your thoughts are from the enemy or the Lord, ask yourself, "Are these thoughts I would *choose* to have?" If you answer no, then they are probably from your enemy.

Don't live with confusion or mental oppression. You never have to "live as the Gentiles do, in the futility of their thinking. They are darkened in their understanding and separated from the life of God because of the ignorance that is in them due to the hardening of their hearts" (Ephesians 4:17-18). Instead, ask God to give you clarity and knowledge. Ask Him to give you ears to hear His voice. Ask Him to make you a good listener.

Almighty God, help me to be a good listener to Your voice speaking to my heart. I don't want to drown it out with the noise and busyness of life. Help me to take my every thought captive in obedience to Your Word. Keep me from entertaining unrighteousness in my thought life. Enable me to be diligent in not allowing anything into my mind that does not glorify You. In Jesus' name I pray.

GOD IS *with* YOU

"When you go to war against your enemies and see horses and chariots and an army greater than yours, do not be afraid of them, because the LORD your God, who brought you up out of Egypt, will be with you" (Deuteronomy 20:1).

Prayer is one of your strongest weapons against fear. Imagine how the Israelites must have felt every time they faced nation after nation as they made their way toward the promised land. God required that they rely on His strength, not on their numbers or weapons or skills or any other human power they had. He seemed to delight in making sure that they were weaker than the nations they faced so that His power could be revealed in their victories. And when the Israelites believed Him and followed His instructions, God's power was always revealed.

What "wars" are you facing right now? What impossible circumstances are making you draw back in fear? Take them to the Lord in prayer. Think of all the times in your life when God has been faithful to you. It will reinforce your confidence that God will take you through the next "battle" just as He has seen you through past difficulties. When the Israelites thought back on their dramatic rescue from Egypt and remembered God's faithfulness to them, they renewed their strength to face the challenges ahead. Pray that God will open your eyes to all the ways He has upheld you in the past. Ask Him to give you fresh faith to fearlessly face the next battle.

Almighty God, I rely on You to lead me through every challenge and battle in my life. Help me to never operate out of fear in the face of what seems like impossible circumstances. Just as You have helped me in the past, I know You will continue to help me in the future. I praise You for the great things You will do, and thank You that Your presence is always with me.
In Jesus' name I pray.

MOVING *in the* SPIRIT

"And I will put my Spirit in you and move you to follow my decrees and be careful to keep my laws" (Ezekiel 36:27).

We all have to do things we don't want to do. Even in the best of jobs, there are still aspects we don't enjoy. When we do things we don't like simply because we know we need to do them, it builds character in us, makes us disciplined, and forms us into leaders God can trust. Besides, there's always a price to pay when we forsake the things we *need* to do in order to do only the things we *feel* like doing. We must be willing to make sacrifices for the blessings we want.

When we ask God for it, He will give us the discipline we need in order to do all the tasks that are distasteful to us. When God asks us to do something, He also promises to equip us to carry it out. "The one who calls you is faithful and he will do it" (1 Thessalonians 5:24). Look at the men and women in Scripture whom God singled out for extraordinary assignments. Moses was in his senior years, David was only a shepherd boy, and Jesus' mother, Mary, was most likely just a teenager. None of them felt qualified for the work to which God called them, and yet they responded in obedience and faith, and God enabled them to do what they needed to do.

God has promised to put His Spirit within you. Wherever you go and whatever tasks are before you, you have the pledge of His powerful guidance. But you have to be continually tapped into Him. You have to be in constant communication with Him in order to be plugged into His power. You have to be moving in the Spirit in order to do all He has for you to do.

*Lord, lead me by the power of Your Holy Spirit so that I
will always obey Your Word and follow Your laws. Give
me the discipline I need to do what I must do. Thank You
that You have put Your Holy Spirit within me to guide
me in all things. Help me to follow Your leading and
not run ahead or behind chasing after my own ways.
In Jesus' name I pray.*

HUMBLED *in* HIS PRESENCE

∽ Read and Consider ∽
1 Kings 8:22-30,56-61

*"But will God really dwell on earth? The heavens, even
the highest heaven, cannot contain you. How much
less this temple I have built!" (1 Kings 8:27).*

The magnificent temple was finally complete. All the furnishings
had been installed. The ark of the Lord was in the Most Holy
Place. Then, before the ribbon cutting celebration could proceed,
God's presence in the form of a dark cloud filled the temple. The
huge crowd must have been awestruck.

Solomon raised his arms toward heaven, silencing the assembly,
and began his prayer. After a brief acknowledgment of his father,
David's, (and his) role within God's plan, Solomon asked a wonderful
rhetorical question: "How can this temple hold You?" He knew
that despite its glory, the temple could not contain God, since even
the highest heaven could not contain Him. It was one of the most
magnificent structures any human had ever created to honor God,
yet the true glory of the temple did not lie in the skill of the builders
but in the *presence of God.*

When you come before God in prayer, one way you know you're
in His presence is your sense of humility before Him. You can't
be full of yourself and filled with His Spirit at the same time. You
will always be humbled whenever you realize that this awesome
God—whom the heavens cannot contain—is willing to come and
live *inside you* through His Holy Spirit.

∽

*Dear Lord, I thank You for Your presence in my
life. I am thankful and humbled that You—through
Your Holy Spirit—live inside me. Help me to never
be full of myself, but rather to always be freshly filled
with more of You each day. Help me to have a sense
of Your presence, especially as I read Your Word
and pray and live in obedience to Your ways.
In Jesus' name I pray.*

WHY PRAYER WORKS

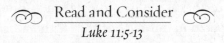

*"I tell you, though he will not get up and give him the bread
because he is his friend, yet because of the man's boldness he
will get up and give him as much as he needs" (Luke 11:8).*

This parable about prayer gives us some insight into how Jesus
expects us to pray—Boldly! Understanding why prayer works
can help us to pray boldly. Here are a few reasons we can pray with
confidence:

Prayer works because of what Jesus did. When we pray we are
applying Jesus' victory through the cross, taking the rule away
from Satan and establishing the rule of God. In that way we stop
the devil's work and establish the Lord's will. We take things that
are wrong and make them right. When we become believers, God
doesn't take us to heaven right away—and for a good reason. There
are things He has for us to do on earth. He wants us to expose
the enemy's lies and proclaim God's truth. He wants us to bring
down the enemy's strongholds and set the captives free. He wants
us to bring health where there is sickness, love where there is fear,
forgiveness where there is condemnation, revelation where there is
spiritual blindness, and wholeness where there is a fracture in our
lives. God's Word reveals that this can be accomplished when we
pray. When we understand this, it's easier to pray boldly.

Prayer works because we live God's way. In order to get our prayers
answered, we need to walk in obedience to God's laws. "We have
confidence before God and receive from him anything we ask,
because we obey his commands and do what pleases him" (1 John
3:21-22). You may be thinking that this is enough to disqualify you

right there. How can you always do what pleases God? But God is merciful in this too, because we can pray about these issues as well. He will even help us to obey if we ask Him. Remember, the answers to our prayers are not earned by our obedience. But our privilege to pray boldly is rooted in our relationship with Father God. And He has called us to walk as obedient children.

Prayer works because we don't hesitate to ask. God wants us to be bold in our asking. Being bold isn't stomping into the throne room of God and demanding what we think we deserve, but it is recognizing that God wants to do above and beyond what we think possible (Ephesians 3:20). This knowledge makes us courageous to ask God to do great things in us, through us, and around us. Jesus' story about the man who persisted in asking for bread from his neighbor suggests that we not only ask persistently but boldly as well.

I once had someone tell me they prayed only about the "big stuff" because they didn't want to waste any of their prayers on small things, as if God only allows us a certain number of prayer requests per lifetime, so we had better make our prayers count. God says we are to ask continually—to pray without ceasing. He wants us to pray *all* the time about *everything*. God is always ready to hear from us. He wants us to ask because He wants to answer.

Lord, help me to be bold and persistent in prayer. I don't want to be arrogant or presumptuous, as if You owe me anything, but rather to be confident in what Jesus accomplished on the cross that took away Satan's rule and established Your own. Help me to have great faith that You hear my prayers and will answer in Your way and time. Help me to be confident enough to ask for great things, knowing You will answer in a great way even if it's not the way I thought it would be. In Jesus' name I pray.

GOD IS *on* YOUR SIDE

"'Be strong and courageous. Do not be afraid or discouraged
because of the king of Assyria and the vast army with
him, for there is a greater power with us than with
him. With him is only the arm of flesh, but with us is
the LORD *our God to help us and to fight our battles.'*
And the people gained confidence from what Hezekiah
the king of Judah said" (2 Chronicles 32:7-8).

King Hezekiah knew the king of Assyria was going to attack Jerusalem. It was only a matter of time. So he gathered his advisors and worked hard to build up his defenses and prepare the city. Then he gathered the people and reminded them that no matter the size of the army against them, God was bigger. "And the people gained confidence." By acknowledging and remembering who God was, they all found strength.

It's not wrong to be afraid of what you see *could* happen. That's realism. What *is* wrong is to not seek God's help immediately and humble yourself in worship before Him. Among other things, our praise reminds the enemy of who God is and how well we know Him. Always keep in mind that the enemy does not want you to worship God. So every time you attempt to build an altar to God in your life, the enemy will try to stop you.

Have you faced any frightening opposition in your life lately? Have you felt the enemy of your soul waging a full attack against you? Are you sometimes overwhelmed at how little strength and power you feel in the midst of it all? Don't worry; pray, and remember, "The one who is in you is greater than the one who is in the world" (1 John 4:4).

When King Hezekiah faced a strong enemy, he told his people the truth—God is greater. Keep in mind that when you acknowledge and praise God in the midst of enemy opposition, there is far more power with you than there is with the enemy.

Thank You, Lord, that You are with me in everything
that I face. No matter what comes against me, You are
greater and more powerful. I ask You to be with me in
the things I face today. I praise You and Your greatness
in the midst of all that seems large and looming in my
life. I know Your power with me will always be far
stronger than that of the enemy who opposes me.
In Jesus' name I pray.

GOD WILL POUR OUT *as* MUCH *as* YOU CAN RECEIVE

Read and Consider
2 Kings 4:1-7

"Elisha said, 'Go around and ask all your neighbors for empty jars. Don't ask for just a few. Then go inside and shut the door behind you and your sons. Pour oil into all the jars, and as each is filled, put it to one side'" (2 Kings 4:3-4).

The widow came to Elisha for help because her sons were about to be sold into slavery to cover her debts. When he asked her what she had in her house, she said all she had was one jar of oil. He instructed her to borrow empty jars, *but not just a few.*

The widow didn't know what God would do with these empty jars; she only knew He asked her to gather *many.* This woman's faith would be measured by how many jars she collected.

God took what the widow had in her one jar and multiplied it to fill all the containers she had borrowed and brought into her house. She was then able to sell the oil and pay her debts.

God will take what you have and multiply it to meet your needs as well. But how well are you able to contain all God has for you? Do you have faith enough to embrace the big things God wants to do in your life? If not, ask Him to give you big faith, and then determine to shut the door on doubt.

∽

Heavenly Father, give me a vision of all You want to do in my life. Help me to not think too small when I pray. I want to be available to whatever You have for me and

*not limit Your blessings by being unprepared to receive
them. Enlarge my heart and mind to understand how
You can take what I have and expand it beyond what
I can imagine. Help me to not stop praying too soon.
In Jesus' name I pray.*

Thank God *for* His Mercy *to* You

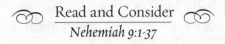

Read and Consider
Nehemiah 9:1-37

*"But in your great mercy you did not put an end
to them or abandon them, for you are a gracious
and merciful God" (Nehemiah 9:31).*

Nehemiah and the people of Israel had just accomplished an impossible mission. They had rebuilt the massive walls of Jerusalem in record time. Against all odds and opposition they had succeeded. Now it was time for another kind of rebuilding—accepting and applying God's written instructions for His people. Nehemiah chapter 8 describes a national Bible study of sorts, as Ezra reintroduced God's law to the people. Chapter 9 records the effects of God's Word settling into the hearts and minds of God's people. They arrived at a clear understanding of how far they had drifted from God's ways, and so they gathered for a great service of national repentance and worship.

In God's presence, the people reviewed their history, highlighting the repeated sins of the nation as well as God's repeated mercy and faithfulness. This review wasn't to inform God, but to demonstrate to themselves that they understood how things had come to be. They were standing as a small remnant of a great nation that had been humbled under God's just judgment. In God's mercy they had returned to their land. Their very existence was an amazing tribute to God's faithfulness. Despite everything His people had done to violate the covenants He had made with them in the past, God had kept His word. They knew God was faithful, so they dared to start over.

Their prayer of confession offers us a good example. We need to review our spiritual history in prayer from time to time. Particularly when we have followed the Lord for a long time, we need to trace the journey we have traveled with Him. Perhaps we hesitate to do this because we realize our history with God is like the Israelites' was—full of our failures as well as God's faithfulness. God certainly takes no pleasure in our review of sins unless it leads us to repentance and a clearer understanding of all He has done to guard and guide us along the way. Thank God for all the times He has shown His mercy and grace to you.

Lord, I am aware every day of Your great mercy toward me. Thank You that You have never judged me according to what I have deserved. Your grace toward me is beyond comprehension. Thank You that You will never forsake me. Help me to never forsake You in any way either. I pray that my attitude will always be right before You, and I will never take Your mercy for granted. In Jesus' name I pray.

BEING FAITHFUL *in* PRAYER

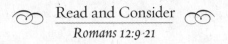

Read and Consider

Romans 12:9-21

"Be joyful in hope, patient in affliction,
faithful in prayer" (Romans 12:12).

Aconsistent prayer life requires faithfulness. We have to take the time, maintain focus, and commit to not allowing too much time to go by in between each prayer. And we need to not grow weary when our prayers seem to go unanswered.

The words Paul wrote to the Romans offer us some insight into the expectations that God places on our prayer lives. God doesn't require eloquence. He doesn't ask that our prayers be a certain length or that we pray a certain number of times every day. God asks that we be "faithful in prayer."

So what does faithfulness in prayer mean? It means making prayer an ongoing, consistent part of our lives. It's being diligent to set aside time for prayer. It's developing a sense of awe and stillness before God. It's praying for someone when we promised we would. It's taking time to sit before God and ask for His direction rather than rushing through each decision. It's seeking out God's purpose in our lives rather than merely reacting to our circumstances. It's continuing to come to Him even when we don't feel that we're getting any answers. When we are faithful to pray—to talk to our heavenly Father—we establish intimacy with Him. That alone is reason enough to be faithful in prayer.

Lord, make me to be a person of powerful prayer. Teach
me how to be a prayer warrior who is always faithful

*to pray according to Your will. I don't want to be
someone who prays sporadically, but rather a person so
filled with joy and hope that I anticipate great things
resulting from each prayer. Help me to have such strong
faith that I keep on praying without giving up.
In Jesus' name I pray.*

GOD HEARS WHEN YOU CALL

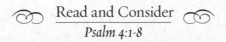

Read and Consider
Psalm 4:1-8

"Know that the LORD has set apart the godly for himself;
the LORD will hear when I call to him" (Psalm 4:3).

Psalms is one of the most encouraging books in all of Scripture. There is no emotion we can experience, whether elation or depression, guilt or gladness, that we won't find first expressed in Psalms. This book is the ancient hymnal of the Israelites, and the 150 psalms contained in its pages are a combination of prayer, poetry, and praise. When you don't know what to say to God, pray the psalms back to Him!

Whenever you feel *desperate* to know that God is close and that He is hearing your prayers and will answer you, read this verse again. Remember that God hears the prayers of the godly. The Hebrew word for *godly* is often translated "saints." God sees you as a saint, and He has set you apart for Himself. If you've accepted Christ as your Savior, you are a saint, a child of God, set apart for His glory (Romans 8:16-17). Yet even though we know this is how God sees us, there are times when we don't feel close to God—times when He feels far away and our prayers seem to go no further than the ceiling.

Your prayers may appear to go unanswered for many reasons. God may simply be giving you the answer that you are to wait. It could be that some sin in your life is clouding your communication with Him. Isaiah wrote, "Your iniquities have separated you from your God; your sins have hidden his face from you, so that he will not hear" (Isaiah 59:2). Make sure that nothing in your life is acting as a barrier between you and God.

Be encouraged! As God's child, you have His ear. Stay close, and He promises to hear when you call.

*Thank You, Lord, that I am a child of Yours, set apart
for Your purpose and glory, and that You hear my prayers.
When I pray, help me to have the peace of knowing You
have heard my prayer and will answer it according to Your
will and in Your perfect timing. Show me if there is ever
anything in my life that would become a barrier between me
and You causing my prayers to go unanswered. I will confess
that immediately and separate myself from that hindrance.
In Jesus' name I pray.*

INVITING GOD'S PRESENCE
and FORGIVENESS

∽ Read and Consider ∽
2 Chronicles 6:12-42

*"Now, my God, may your eyes be open and your ears
attentive to the prayers offered in this place. Now
arise, O LORD God, and come to your resting place,
you and the ark of your might. May your priests, O
LORD God, be clothed with salvation, may your saints
rejoice in your goodness" (2 Chronicles 6:40-41).*

Solomon's workers had completed the temple construction. David, Solomon's father and predecessor, had gathered the materials, but Solomon was charged with completing the actual structure. Such attention to detail was given to this process that it took seven years to complete the majestic temple. The walls and furniture were covered with gold. The king of Tyre himself shipped the lumber in from Lebanon.

Yet even with all its finery, it wasn't the temple building that prompted Solomon's thoughtful prayer here. It was God's glorious presence filling that temple. Finally there was a place for God to dwell more permanently among His people. Since the nation's whole identity was based on its relationship with God and His blessing, this was a very significant moment.

In light of that, it's interesting to really listen to Solomon's prayer. Rather than a formal prayer laced with high and holy phrases, it is a very down-to-earth prayer filled with the tough stuff of real life. Solomon covered the gamut of life situations that these people were going to face as they worshiped for—what he hopes will be—many centuries at this temple.

After describing all the possible tragedies that could happen, Solomon's prayer was, in essence, "Be with us." No matter how the people might stray, he wanted God to hear their prayers of repentance and forgive them. He wanted God's presence.

We should pray the same way—inviting God's presence to dwell in us and to forgive us whenever we stray from His ways.

Holy Father, there is nothing more important than Your presence in my life. Help me to be a holy dwelling place for Your Spirit. Forgive me of all sin and cleanse my heart of all unrighteousness. Nothing is more comforting to me than to know You are with me, no matter what is happening in my life. Keep me from ever doing anything to separate myself from You in any way.
In Jesus' name I pray.

FINDING GOD'S
FORGIVENESS *and* LOVE

∽∽ Read and Consider ∽∽
Hosea 14

*"Take words with you and return to the LORD. Say to
him: 'Forgive all our sins and receive us graciously, that
we may offer the fruit of our lips'" (Hosea 14:2).*

The book of Hosea is an unusual love story of a husband, an
unfaithful wife, and a love that forgives and redeems even when
the relationship seems irreparably broken. Put yourself in Hosea's
place. God tells you to take an adulterous wife, give your kids odd
names that represent divine messages, and pay to get your wife back
after she has disgraced herself with other men. Then God instructs
you to forgive her and love her more than before.

Your reaction might be, "Are You joking, God? You want me to
what?" But Hosea didn't question God. Instead, he did exactly as
God said. As a result his life became a beautiful metaphor of God's
love for the unfaithful nation of Israel and for each of us individu-
ally. It parallels God's love for His "bride" (His people) and the
reconciliation that God's true love brings about.

Hosea calls the people of Israel to repentance, to turn back to
God. He even gives them the words to say: "Forgive all our sins and
receive us graciously...for in you the fatherless [we] find compassion"
(14:2-3). These simple but amazing words, when prayed with honesty
and a contrite heart, are as relevant today as they were 2500 years
ago. No matter how faithless we have been, God will be faithful
and just to forgive us (1 John 1:9).

Forgiveness begins when we recognize how sinful and needy
we are. We can't save ourselves, and no amount of money, fame, or

power can save us either. Our only hope is to throw ourselves upon the mercy of our Creator, knowing we don't deserve it. God loves us so much that He paid in blood to redeem us. Jesus Christ, His only Son, gave His life that we might forever have God's compassionate forgiveness.

When you are tired of trying to be good on your own, weary of a life of sin, when your friends and family desert you, when you feel yourself sinking in the quicksand of guilt, lift your voice to God. Ask Him to forgive you for your sins and for trying to do it all on your own. He will wash away your past, start you on a new path, and walk with you. Together, you and He will write your own love story, a story that will last forever.

Dear God, I recognize how sinful and needy I am.
I know I cannot save myself in any way, but You
have saved me in every way. That's why I humble
myself before You, first of all in confession of my sins.
Secondly, I praise You for all You have done for me by
extending Your forgiveness, love, and mercy to me.
I love You above all else and am forever grateful.
In Jesus' name I pray.

KEEP PRAYING NO MATTER WHAT

꧁ Read and Consider ꧂
Habakkuk 1:1-11

"How long, O LORD, must I call for help, but
you do not listen? Or cry out to you, 'Violence!'
but you do not save?" (Habakkuk 1:2).

Isn't it interesting to note that Habakkuk felt the same way about society as Christians feel today? There seems to be no justice upon the wicked.

You might see a situation and wonder, *Where is God in the midst of this? Why do bad things happen to good people? How are the evildoers getting away with cheating, violence, oppression, and perversion?* Habakkuk saw the evil around him, and he cried out to God for answers. He didn't doubt God's omnipotence; rather, he didn't understand why God would allow sin to run rampant in the world. God answered the prophet, telling him exactly what He planned to do.

Today injustice, evil, and sin continue to appear to prosper, but not because God is indifferent. God has a plan. He wants us to partner with Him in this plan by praying. Whenever you feel sad over what you see happening in the world today, pour out your concerns to God in prayer. Pray that you and your fellow believers might be a light in a darkened world, bringing the hope and peace of Jesus to those with whom you interact every day. God will answer those prayers.

Habakkuk knew that he would need to persevere no matter what. We must do the same. "Though the fig tree does not bud and there are no grapes on the vines, though the olive crop fails and the fields produce no food, though there are no sheep in the pen and no cattle in the stalls, yet I will rejoice in the LORD, I will be joyful in God my Savior" (3:17-18). We must learn to say, "No matter how bad it gets, Lord, I will be joyful and not stop praying until Your will is done on earth."

Lord, help me to have the understanding and faith I need to keep praying and not give up if my prayers are not answered right away. I know Your ways are perfect. Help me to not become discouraged in the time of waiting for Your help, but rather to continue praying until I see Your will done in all the things You put on my heart to pray about. In Jesus' name I pray.

LET TIME *with* GOD TAKE *the* PLACE *of* WORRYING

⤜ Read and Consider ⤛
Luke 12:22-34

*"Who of you by worrying can add a single
hour to his life?" (Luke 12:25).*

N one of us can add a single moment to our lives by worrying. In fact, the opposite is probably more true; we actually *lose* life when we worry. We are wasting the time we spend worrying, and we may be causing health problems that could ultimately shorten our lives.

Jesus tells us to refuse to worry because no matter what problems we have, He has already overcome them. "In this world you will have trouble. But take heart! I have overcome the world" (John 16:33). We can find freedom from anxiety just by spending time with Him. "When anxiety was great within me, your consolation brought joy to my soul" (Psalm 94:19).

When you are anxious, it means you aren't trusting God to take care of you. But He will prove His faithfulness if you run to Him. "Do not set your heart on what you will eat or drink; do not worry about it. For the pagan world runs after all such things, and your Father knows that you need them. But seek his kingdom, and these things will be given to you as well" (Luke 12:29-31).

God says we don't need to be anxious about *anything;* we just need to pray about *everything.* So instead of worrying, actively bring your cares to Him. Prayer is not empty, powerless, wishful thinking. It is a powerful connection with the One who is the source of our comfort, strength, and hope. So take your worries about the future to the One who holds your future in His hands.

*Dear God, I pray You would help me to stop worrying
about things and start trusting You more. I know the
time I waste by worrying is better spent in Your presence
listening for Your voice speaking to my heart. You are
my source of strength, hope, love, peace, and rest, and I
want to be connected with You and not the things that
worry me. I surrender all that concerns me into Your
hands knowing You have the answer to each problem.
In Jesus' name I pray.*

The Antidote for Fear

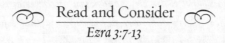
"With praise and thanksgiving they sang to the LORD: 'He is good; his love to Israel endures forever.' And all the people gave a great shout of praise to the LORD, because the foundation of the house of the LORD was laid" (Ezra 3:11).

The people of Judah had been exiled. Jerusalem and its temple were in ruins. Outsiders had taken over the land—people who did not understand or revere the customs of the Jewish nation. So when the first Jews returned from their exile, they were fearful and a bit intimidated by the people around them. But they knew they must rebuild, and so they began. It was a slow and arduous process, but finally the foundation of the temple was laid.

And then the people pulled out all the stops, praising God, singing songs, shouting, and playing trumpets and cymbals. They were so *loud* that all the foreign neighbors heard them.

When you're struggling, or doubting, or fearful, or feel as if your foundation has crumbled, don't ever underestimate the power of praise! Don't just think about it. Do it. Pull out all the stops. Make praise your *first* response to fearful situations in your life. God wants us to praise Him at all times, but especially when we are afraid or discouraged. When we do, not only will He take away our fear, but He will also give us joy (Psalm 34:1-5).

Fear will tell you things that are not God's truth for your life. Fear denies that God's presence is powerful and fully active in your life. It cancels all hope and faith in God's desire to work in your behalf. But the truth is that faith, prayer, praise, and the Word of God will conquer your every fear.

*Lord, I praise Your name. You are almighty and far
more powerful than any opposition of the enemy. Your
presence in my life is greater than anything I fear. I
know faith in You and in Your Word will defeat
all the works of evil threatening my life. With Your
help I will not dwell on my problems, but instead
I will praise You and Your name continually.
In Jesus' name I pray.*

MOVING INTO *the* FREEDOM
GOD HAS *for* US

∽ Read and Consider ∽
Galatians 5:1-15

"It is for freedom that Christ has set us free. Stand firm, then, and do not let yourselves be burdened again by a yoke of slavery" (Galatians 5:1).

Did you inherit your mother's eyes or your father's nose? How about your grandmother's talent for art or your grandfather's gift of music?

There are many physical characteristics, gifts, abilities, and talents that we can inherit from our parents and grandparents. Unfortunately, though, we can also inherit character qualities that aren't so enviable—things like a bad temper, a propensity for lying, negativity, unforgiveness, perfectionism, or pride. These and other entrenched characteristics that have a spiritual base can also be passed along from our parents to us, and from us to our children. In a particular family there may be a tendency toward such things as addiction, suicide, depression, rejection, or being accident-prone—all mistakenly accepted as "fate" or "the way I am."

Some of what we accept about ourselves and our lives are actually family bondages, for children can inherit the consequences of their ancestors' sins. "I, the LORD your God, am a jealous God, punishing the children for the sin of the fathers to the third and fourth generation of those who hate me" (Exodus 20:5). This Scripture is referring to people who don't walk in a loving relationship with God, but how many of our ancestors didn't walk with God and how many times have we been less than lovingly obedient to Him?

Galatians warns us not to be burdened again by a yoke of slavery, or bondage. If it is not possible as a believer to become entangled again with a yoke of bondage, why does the Bible warn us about it? The answer is, even though Jesus set us free from sin, we can still make choices that put us back into bondage to it.

Sometimes we accept certain tendencies toward sin in ourselves, without realizing that we don't have to. We can say no to them in our lives. Sometimes we carry on a family tradition that we shouldn't and it affects our children. Unlike physical traits, tendencies toward sin are something we don't have to receive as an inheritance from our parents. That's because these tendencies are nothing more than the unquestioned acceptance of a firmly entrenched lie of the enemy. He wants us to believe that we are not a new creation in Christ and that we have not been set free from our old nature. He wants us to think that because Dad (or Grandpa) drank too much, cheated on his wife, or abused his family with his anger, that this is just the way things are done in our family. But we can choose to break away from these old familial habits through prayer and the power of the Holy Spirit. And when we see things we don't like about ourselves reflected in our children, we can pray for them to be set free of that tendency as well. In Jesus' name we can be set free from any family bondage, and by the power of the Holy Spirit we can refuse to allow it any place in the lives of our children.

Lord, help me to stand firm in the freedom You have secured for me. Thank You, Jesus, that You gave Your life so that I could be set free from the yoke of slavery to the enemy of my soul. Help me to not become entangled in it again. Make me aware when I am allowing bondage back into my life from which You have set me free. In Jesus' name I pray.

WANTING GOD'S WILL

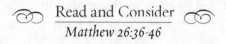

Read and Consider
Matthew 26:36-46

*"Going a little farther, he fell with his face to the
ground and prayed, 'My Father, if it is possible,
may this cup be taken from me. Yet not as I
will, but as you will'"* (Matthew 26:39).

I t's important to pray for God's will to be done in our lives, but how
do we align our own desires and will with what God wants? How
do we learn to *want* God's plan for us more than we want our own?

Jesus' passionate prayer in the garden of Gethsemane is the
greatest model for us of praying with absolute honesty and total
submission. He knew He would be arrested, tortured, and put to
death as part of God's plan of redemption for the world. The "cup"
that He was about to drink was the cup of divine wrath for the sins
of humanity, and He was about to take upon Himself the penalty
for that sin. He anticipated the physical pain and suffering as well
as the emotional agony of being separated from His Father, and He
asked that this cup of suffering be taken away. The intensity of this
prayer gives us a glimpse of Jesus' humanity. If it wasn't going to be
painful, He would not have agonized to this extent.

You and I face times that aren't easy. We look ahead and sense
God saying, "Stay in this difficult marriage," "Love that rebellious
child," "Return kindness to that belligerent boss." Just like Jesus did,
we can ask God to remove the cup of pain from our lives, to give
us an easier way out. But like Jesus, we have to also say: "Yet not as
I will, but as You will." The easy way may not be the best way. The
easy way is often not the way God has for you.

God wants us to pray about all things, but He wants us to pray according to His will. That's why it's important to ask God to reveal His will to us and help us pray accordingly. When we don't know what God's will is, we should always include in our prayer, "Lord, let Your perfect will be done in this situation."

Heavenly Father, more than anything I want Your will to be done in my life. Even though I want You to take away all my pain and suffering, and I want all of Your blessings, and I want things to turn out the way I want them to, above all I want Your will to be accomplished and not my own. Reveal Your will to me and help me to pray and act accordingly. In Jesus' name I pray.

GET PERSONAL *with* GOD

*"Therefore the LORD was very angry with Israel and
said, 'Because this nation has violated the covenant that
I laid down for their forefathers and has not listened
to me, I will no longer drive out before them any of the
nations Joshua left when he died'" (Judges 2:20-21).*

After years of struggle to get to the promised land, the nation of
Israel fell away from the Lord who had led them there. Why?
Because they did not maintain their own personal connection to
Him. Relying on the faith of their fathers wasn't enough to sustain
them, and they turned to other gods.

The same principle holds true for us. We cannot rely on other
people's faith, or even our own past experiences with God, to sustain
our current relationship with Him. We must maintain a living,
dynamic, active relationship with Him through our prayer life and
Scripture reading in order to know Him at an intimate level.

Prayer is about so much more than just making requests or getting
advice. It is our avenue to knowing and being known by the God of
the universe. Although He already knows us completely, we don't
have any way of experiencing that reality if we do not connect with
Him in a personal way.

God created you, and He desires to be part of your life. He doesn't
want you to fall into temptations and dangers as the Israelites did.
Make sure that you maintain a consistent prayer life and guard
against riding on past experiences with Him. Doing so can get you
into dangerous territory.

*Father God, I don't want to ever fall away from You by
neglecting to spend time in Your Word and in prayer.
I want to always be moving into a closer walk with You.
Help me to know You better and to become more and more
like You. I don't want to get off the path You have for me
by falling into temptation, sin, or laziness. I want, instead,
to have a new and deeper experience with You every day.
In Jesus' name I pray.*

How Can I Be Holy?

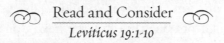
*"Speak to the entire assembly of Israel and
say to them: 'Be holy because I, the LORD
your God, am holy'" (Leviticus 19:2).*

What do you think about when you think of holiness? Do you think of someone who is perfect and untouchable? What do you think about your own holiness? Do you ever wonder, *How can I be holy?* Throughout Israel's history, holiness was a major issue. As the people's holiness went, so went the state of the nation. Their spiritual strength and their political strength seemed to go hand in hand. In the days of the good King Jehoshaphat, Judah actually won a battle because the people marched before the army singing and praising God for the "splendor of his holiness" (2 Chronicles 20:1-27).

When you think about how to be holy as God is holy, consider this good news: God wants to share His holiness with you. He doesn't stand over you, wagging an index finger in your face like a judgmental teacher saying, "You be holy right now!" Instead, He offers His own holiness to you. He asks you to partake of His holiness.

In Psalm 29, David encouraged us to offer praise to God for His strength and glory and holiness. When we do that, amazing things happen. Because we take the time and attention to see the splendor and beauty of God's holiness, we take on that beauty. The more we lift our heads and hearts to God in praise, the more God is reflected in our faces and in our behavior.

Remember how Moses' face was radiant when he came down from being in the presence of God (Exodus 34:29-35)? When you worship God, you are coming in contact with the beauty of His holiness and allowing that to make you beautifully holy and wonderfully whole.

That's why your time in prayer shouldn't always be squeezed in between running from one thing to the next. You need time with God to really engage and bask in His presence, allowing Him to conform you and remold you in His image. Each time you do that, you become more holy, more like Him.

Dear God, I worship You for Your greatness and
goodness. I praise You for Your holiness. As I worship
You, I pray Your holiness will be imparted to me. Help
me to take on the beauty of Your holiness as I spend
time in Your presence. Enable me to become more
like You so that Your holiness will make me whole.
In Jesus' name I pray.

THIRSTING AFTER GOD

Read and Consider
Psalm 63:1-11

*"O God, you are my God, earnestly I seek you; my soul
thirsts for you, my body longs for you, in a dry and
weary land where there is no water" (Psalm 63:1).*

If you were lost in the desert without anything to eat or drink,
you would seek food and water anywhere you could find it, even
if it wasn't good for you. You wouldn't care how many impurities
it had in it or how bad it tasted because you want to survive. But
God has so much more for you than just survival.

What do *you* hunger and thirst for right now? Is it more of the
Lord?

When King David hungered and thirsted for the Lord, he said,
"As the deer pants for streams of water, so my soul pants for you,
O God. My soul thirsts for God, for the living God. When can I
go and meet with God?" (42:1-2). He wanted the Lord more than
anything else. God's presence was food and water to him.

Have you ever been that thirsty for God? Sometimes we don't
experience that deep thirst until we know what it's like to wander
in the desert of our own desires. We grab for what the world has to
offer only to discover that it leaves us empty.

Jesus once said, "If anyone is thirsty, let him come to me and
drink. Whoever believes in me, as the Scripture has said, streams
of living water will flow from within him" (John 7:37-38). Jesus
was quoting from an invitation given in the Old Testament book
of Isaiah, in which the prophet recorded these words: "Come, all
you who are thirsty, come to the waters" (Isaiah 55:1). When we

quench our spiritual thirst in the Lord, His Spirit will flow *through* us, and streams of living water will flow *from* us.

Drink deeply of all that God has for you in His Word, in His presence, and in prayer and praise, and you will never be thirsty again!

> *Lord God, above all else I desire Your presence in my life. I long for more of You the way I long for water in the dry heat of summer. I come to You to quench my spiritual thirst as only You can do. Flow Your rivers of living water into me so they can revive my soul and then flow through me to a dry and thirsty world.*
> *In Jesus' name I pray.*

BY HIS SPIRIT

"So he said to me, 'This is the word of the LORD to Zerubbabel: "Not by might nor by power, but by my Spirit," says the LORD Almighty'" (Zechariah 4:6).

Zerubbabel was given a huge responsibility: to rebuild the temple in Jerusalem. While the prophets encouraged him in this task, it was Zerubbabel's sole responsibility to see it through to completion. How inadequate he must have felt!

Every time you feel you are unable to do what God has called you to do, when you feel as though you don't have what it takes to move into the life God has for you, worship is the way to respond. First of all, be grateful that you feel the way you do because that means you are humble and dependent on God. Rejoice if you feel inadequate to the task because that means you are going to have to depend on God to enable you to do it. And He will, because "the one who calls you is faithful and he will do it" (1 Thessalonians 5:24).

You don't have to make your life happen; you just have to worship God and let *Him* make it happen. You don't have to strive to figure out your purpose; you have to strive to know God, for *He* knows your purpose. Your praise will illuminate the path by which God will guide you into your future and the purpose He has for you. You won't accomplish it; He will. Not by might or power, but by His Spirit.

Almighty God, I acknowledge I cannot do all You have called me to do, except that Your Spirit enables me to do

*it. I depend on You to help me get where I need to go. I
worship You as the light of my life who illuminates my path
and guides my every step. I praise You as the all-powerful
God of the universe for whom nothing is too hard.
In Jesus' name I pray.*

SEEING *the* POWER *of* GOD *at* WORK

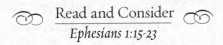
"I pray also that the eyes of your heart may be
enlightened in order that you may know the hope
to which he has called you, the riches of his glorious
inheritance in the saints, and his incomparably great
power for us who believe" (Ephesians 1:18-19).

The power of God is at work in our lives and in the world around us wherever He is invited. So if you ever find yourself thinking that you are not seeing His power manifesting in your life as much as you would like, then perhaps you have not invited Him into your situation with as much fervency as *He* would like. The Holy Spirit never forces Himself upon us. He waits for our invitation.

You can only move in the power of God's Spirit if you have first received Jesus as Savior. You need to "know this love that surpasses knowledge—that you may be filled to the measure of all the fullness of God" (Ephesians 3:19). When you have Jesus as ruler of your life, you will come to know Him as the one "who is able to do immeasurably more than all we ask or imagine, according to his power that is at work within us" (3:20). Because of His Holy Spirit in us—His power in us—He can do more in our lives than we can even think to ask for.

Once you receive Jesus and have the Holy Spirit in you, He will begin to work in your life as you pray. The more you pray—or seek God's presence—the more the Holy Spirit will guide and teach you. Jesus said, "The Counselor, the Holy Spirit, whom the Father will send in my name, will teach you all things and will remind you of everything I have said to you" (John 14:26). When you acknowledge the Holy Spirit and then invite Him to move in you freely, He will. You will see His power manifest.

God *wants* us to witness His power at work in the world. He wants us to understand "his incomparably great power for us who believe" (1:19). He desires that we know this power that raised Jesus "from the dead and seated him at his right hand in the heavenly realms, far above all rule and authority, power and dominion, and every title that can be given" (1:20-21). He wants us to understand that Jesus is not weak toward us, but powerful among us (2 Corinthians 13:3). He wants us to understand that though "he was crucified in weakness, yet he lives by God's power," and even though we are also weak, we live by the power of God too (2 Corinthians 13:4). God wants us to see that "we have not received the spirit of the world but the Spirit who is from God, that we may understand what God has freely given us" (1 Corinthians 2:12).

Invite God to open the eyes of your heart and understanding, so that you will be able to see Him and His power at work in you, in your life, and in the world around you.

Dear God, I pray that the eyes of my heart will be opened
to see the hope to which You have called me. Help me
to understand my true, glorious inheritance. Enable
me to comprehend the magnitude of Your power
on my behalf because I believe in You. I seek
more of Your presence and Your power so that I
can see them clearly manifested in my life.
In Jesus' name I pray.

GOD'S PLANS STILL REQUIRE PRAYER *on* OUR PART

⧽ Read and Consider ⧼
Jeremiah 29:4-14

*"'For I know the plans I have for you,' declares the
LORD, 'plans to prosper you and not to harm you, plans
to give you hope and a future'" (Jeremiah 29:11).*

Jeremiah had some good news and some bad news from God for
the people. The bad news was extremely bad. They would spend
70 years in captivity in Babylon (29:10). The good news was that
God would bring His people home in the end. He had plans for
them—plans to prosper and not harm them, plans to give them
hope and a future. But that still meant that an entire generation
would come and go before the hopeful promise in Jeremiah 29:11
would come true.

Sometimes God's plans can take a long time to come to pass.
(You probably know that already.) And in those long waiting times,
we can lose heart or get discouraged. That's why it's important to
remember that a future filled with hope and blessing doesn't just
happen automatically. There are things we need to do.

The first thing you need to do is to seek God and pray about your
future. "Then you will call upon me and come and pray to me, and
I will listen to you. You will seek me and find me when you seek
me with all your heart" (29:12-13).

The second thing you need to do is to be diligent to obey God.
Every step of obedience you take today will take you into the future
God has planned for you. "Whether you turn to the right or to the
left, your ears will hear a voice behind you, saying, 'This is the way;

walk in it'" (Isaiah 30:21). You have to listen for God's voice leading you every step of the way.

The Holy Spirit is God's guarantee to you that He will help you do what you need to do and bring to pass everything He promised. "Having believed, you were marked in him with a seal, the promised Holy Spirit, who is a deposit guaranteeing our inheritance until the redemption of those who are God's possession—to the praise of his glory" (Ephesians 1:13-14).

Every time you seek God and obey Him, every time you pray and listen for His voice, you are investing in your future. God promises that you have a good future and a reason to have hope. Trust Him for both. It may not happen as quickly as you would like, but what God promises He will deliver.

Lord, I thank You that Your plans for me are for good—to
prosper me and give me a future and a hope. Help me
to obey You in every area of my life so that I don't do
anything that would thwart Your plans for my future. I
seek You about my future now and ask You to help me to
hear Your voice leading me into it every step of the way.
In Jesus' name I pray.

The VALUE of TIME ALONE with GOD

∽ Read and Consider ∽
Matthew 14:22-23

"After he had dismissed them, he went up on a mountainside by himself to pray. When evening came, he was there alone" (Matthew 14:23).

Solitude—time alone—means different things to different people. Some have too little of it and treasure times of quiet with no one else around. Others who live alone may feel they have too much of it. "Alone" to them means "lonely."

There are examples throughout the Gospels of the value Jesus placed on solitude. He was surrounded each day by His disciples who He was teaching and training, and also by crowds of people who were hungry for His touch. Although He was fully God, He was also fully human. In order for Jesus to have the strength to minister continually, He had to make prayer a priority. When painful things happened, Jesus handled them by spending time alone with His Father. "When Jesus heard what had happened [the death of John the Baptist], he withdrew by boat privately to a solitary place" (14:13). Jesus was often alone, but never lonely. He was always spending time with God.

We don't have to ever be lonely either. When we are alone, we can be with God. On the other hand, if Jesus depended on regular times away to communicate with God in solitude, how much more do *we* need to make such times of quiet a priority in our lives!

We often speak of "finding" time to be alone with God, but that valuable time has a way of getting lost in the midst of our overcrowded schedules. We must change our focus from trying to *find* time to *making* time. I heard of one mother who paused each day and threw her apron over her head. When the children saw that, they knew it was Mama's time alone with God! It doesn't matter *how* we do it, we just have to do it.

If you find it hard to make time for solitude, remember that your heavenly Father is wanting and waiting to spend time with you. "The LORD your God is with you, he is mighty to save. He will take great delight in you, he will quiet you with his love, he will rejoice over you with singing" (Zephaniah 3:17). Don't keep God waiting.

Whether you are surrounded by a noisy family or you live entirely isolated, take great joy in making time to be alone with God. "Alone" never has to mean "lonely" when you have the Lord in your life!

> *Dear Lord, help me to make the time I need every day*
> *to be alone with You. Escaping all the diversions and*
> *busyness seems to be a constant struggle, and I need a*
> *greater ability to shut out everything and find solitude with*
> *You in prayer. Enable me to secure a place of peace and*
> *quiet so that I can hear Your voice speaking to my heart.*
> *In Jesus' name I pray.*

INQUIRE *of the* LORD

∽ Read and Consider ∽
Joshua 9

*"The men of Israel sampled their provisions but
did not inquire of the* LORD*" (Joshua 9:14).*

This sentence is so brief that it can be easily missed, but it is the key to the entire story: The men of Israel "did not inquire of the LORD."

Joshua should have known better—they were in a war. The Israelites were in the middle of a divine takeover of an entire region. They would need God's guidance every step of the way. But this time the travelers had come a long way. Their food was moldy, their wineskins were old and cracked, and their clothes and sandals were worn out. It didn't occur to Israel's leaders that they were being set up. The Israelites were fooled because they didn't ask for God's guidance in deciding what to do.

Does this sound familiar? Do you ever get yourself into trouble because you fail to ask for God's wisdom and direction? Could you have made a better decision if you had "inquired of the Lord" right there in that office, in the classroom, at the doctor's office, or on that date? The passage implies that if the Israelites *had* asked for God's direction, they would have figured out what was really going on.

God wants to be part of your decisions, big and small. No issue is too insignificant to bring to God. He can see the big picture; you can't. He sees the future; you don't. He wants you to ask Him for guidance in all your daily decisions because He cares about everything that concerns you. He is your heavenly Father, and He wants to be involved in every aspect of your life. He wants to help you avoid the pitfalls that come when you don't consult Him before taking action. Pray every day that His Spirit will guide you in each decision you make.

Father, I pray You would keep me from running off on my own, trying to do what I think is right instead of seeking You about everything so that I will do what I know is right. Help me to not fall into the traps the enemy has laid for me by forgetting to consult You about all things—even the things I think I can handle on my own. In Jesus' name I pray.

Going Directly *to* God

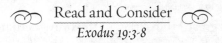
*"So Moses went back and summoned the elders of the
people and set before them all the words the LORD
had commanded him to speak" (Exodus 19:7).*

An intermediary is someone who acts as an agent between two
different parties: a go-between, a mediator. As this passage
reveals, mediation in the form of intercession was clearly a big part
of Moses' role as leader of the nation of Israel. God specifically told
him what to say to the people of Israel, and in turn, Moses brought
their answer back to the Lord.

Throughout history, various religions have taught that people can
only approach God through the intervention of a human mediator.
This was also true for the Jewish people during the times recorded
in the Old Testament. The people could not approach God directly.
Prophets such as Elijah and Elisha arose to speak for the Lord. Kings
wouldn't go off to war without consulting a prophet, who also func-
tioned as a mediator or intercessor. This veil between God and
humanity was symbolized by the thick, heavy curtain that hung in
the Most Holy Place in the tabernacle and later in the temple—a
barrier between a holy God and sinful human beings that only priests
especially anointed for the task could pass through.

With the crucifixion of Jesus Christ, however, all that changed.
At the moment of Christ's death, the curtain in the temple was torn
in two (Mark 15:38), representing the dramatic reality that there
was no longer any obstruction between God and mankind. When
you fully grasp this truth, it will change your life. You do not need
the presence of a human intermediary to take your prayers and

concerns to your heavenly Father. Instead, the book of Hebrews tells us that we can "approach the throne of grace with confidence, so that we may receive mercy and find grace to help us in our time of need" (Hebrews 4:16).

Jesus is your great High Priest—the only mediator you will ever need. "For there is one God and one mediator between God and men, the man Christ Jesus, who gave himself as a ransom for all men" (1 Timothy 2:5-6).

Nothing is wrong with asking others to pray for and with you, but don't hesitate to take the concerns of your heart directly to God. He is waiting!

Thank You, Jesus, that because You gave Your life in sacrifice for mine, the veil of separation has been torn in two and in Your name I can go directly to God in prayer. Help me to remember that I can confidently come to Your throne feeling assured that I will receive Your grace and mercy to help me in my times of need. In Jesus' name I pray.

BE WATCHFUL *in* PRAYER

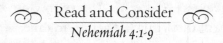

Read and Consider
Nehemiah 4:1-9

*"But we prayed to our God and posted a guard day
and night to meet this threat" (Nehemiah 4:9).*

Working for good in this world will always meet opposition. The enemies of Jerusalem wanted the city to remain in ruins. They were angry when Nehemiah organized the people to rebuild the walls. First they ridiculed, then they threatened, then they planned to attack. The pressure to stop the work grew. Nehemiah prayed against the ridicule and the threats. He trusted God, and he "posted a guard day and night."

There are examples in Scripture when God instructed people to pray and stand back to see Him work (for example, in 2 Kings 19:35, where God wiped out an army laying siege to Jerusalem). But these occasions are rare. Prayer and faith are vital, but so is doing our part.

So how do we know when we should just pray, or when we should pray *and* do something else? The answer is to keep praying, and God will show you. Nehemiah was a man of constant prayer. His ongoing conversations with God gave him insight into what he was to do. At times, God said, "I'll take care of it." At times, God said, "I'll take care of it, but have the people post a guard. They'll all feel better about that." In any case, you can know what to do when you become sensitive to God's guidance as Nehemiah was. Nehemiah and the people never had to fight, but they had to be ready to do so. Their prayers renewed their trust in God; their actions showed that they were willing to have God work things out any way He decided. Whether they had to fight or not, they were not going to stop building the wall, for they were under God's orders. That was a greater motivator for Nehemiah and his people than anything the enemies could throw at them.

We have to be watchful in prayer and always available to do what God has instructed us to do. As we stay in close communication with Him, He will show us what action to take.

> *Dear God, I pray You would help me to be watchful*
> *in prayer so that I am always aware of what I am*
> *supposed to be doing, as well as clearly understanding*
> *what I am not supposed to be doing. Help me to pray*
> *without ceasing so that I can stand guard against*
> *every plan of the enemy to harm or destroy me.*
> *In Jesus' name I pray.*

STAYING DEVOTED *to* PRAYER

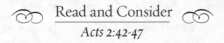

Read and Consider

Acts 2:42-47

*"They devoted themselves to the apostles'
teaching and to the fellowship, to the breaking
of bread and to prayer" (Acts 2:42).*

When Peter preached the gospel to the crowds, they wanted to know what to do. After they had repented of their sins and been baptized, they devoted themselves to the apostles' teaching, to fellowship with one another, to communion, and to prayer. What was important to the new believers in the first century AD is just as important to believers today. Those four things mentioned above are essential for Christians to learn so they can mature and stay close to God. Studying the Bible, spending time with other believers, and partaking of communion are things that often occur in church but can happen anywhere. And they must be made a priority. Prayer is also something we deliberately need to set aside time for because it often gets set aside for other things.

So how can we be devoted to prayer like those early believers? They surely didn't quit their jobs or leave their family responsibilities in order to pray full-time. They went on with their lives in Christ but with a new focus—they were devoted to communication with God! What an awesome thought! They knew God was listening when they had a need or prayed for the needs of others.

We can be devoted to prayer in that same way as well. From the time we get up in the morning to when we go to bed at night, we always have a direct and open line to God. At any time we want, we can talk to God and He will hear and respond.

Devotion to prayer means that we are ready and willing to talk to God in Jesus' name whenever and wherever we feel the need to approach His throne. If we wake up in the middle of the night, we can ask God if there is someone who needs prayer right then. Wherever we are, at any time of day or night, for whatever needs God brings to mind, we can pray knowing God will hear and answer. That's devotion to prayer. That's how to make talking to God a priority.

Dear God, help me to be diligent to study Your Word. Teach me from it so that I can understand it perfectly. Help me to be in communion with other believers so we can be frequently in prayer together. Enable me to maintain that direct line to You by praying constantly and devotedly as You bring things to my mind that need to be covered in prayer. In Jesus' name I pray.

POWERFUL *and* EFFECTIVE PRAYING

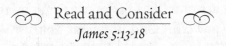
*"Therefore confess your sins to each other and pray for
each other so that you may be healed. The prayer of a
righteous man is powerful and effective" (James 5:16).*

Have you ever wondered, *Are my prayers powerful and effective?
If they aren't, is it because I'm not righteous? After all, James
says the prayers of righteous people are powerful and effective.* If you
ever have doubts about the effectiveness of your prayers because
you haven't seen very many answers to them, then you might be
thinking that you are not good enough to deserve answers. But you
would be mistaken.

Too often when we think about being a righteous person, we
think in terms of our own behavior. The Bible does say that our faith
should work itself out in what we do and the way we live our lives,
but it also teaches that our righteousness comes not because of our
good behavior but because of Christ's sacrifice. The work of Jesus
on the cross and in His resurrection is what gives us righteousness
before God. We are righteous in God's eyes because He sees Jesus'
righteousness in us. We then behave in a righteous manner because
we want to show our love for Jesus by living His way and doing
what He asks us to do.

Too often we think that if our prayers aren't causing sicknesses
to be healed, paralytics to walk, or mountains to be moved, then
they aren't powerful. Too often we think that we have to see such
astounding answers to our prayers in order to prove they are effective.
But the truth is, we often don't get to see the results of our prayers
at all. We don't know the ways in which God is working through

our prayers to touch people or the circumstances of their lives. We don't know how much we have effected or prevented in our own lives through prayer.

Prayer is an act of faith. Our prayers are powerful because we pray them to a powerful God in whom we trust. We just have to pray and trust God to answer in His way and time.

Lord, how grateful I am that my righteousness comes
not because I do everything perfectly, but because You
have done everything perfectly. I am seen as righteous
because of Your great sacrifice on the cross. Help me to
confess my sins not only to You, but also to others who
may be affected so that healing can come to us all. Thank
You for making my prayers powerful and effective.
In Jesus' name I pray.

The HIDDEN POWER *of* PRAISE

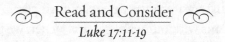

Read and Consider
Luke 17:11-19

*"One of them, when he saw he was healed, came
back, praising God in a loud voice" (Luke 17:15).*

Ten lepers cried out to Jesus to heal them, and He did. But only one of the ten returned and glorified God. How often are we like the other nine? God does something great for us, and we just take it in stride and don't fall down on our face at His feet and thank Him for it. We often do that with healing, even when it is an answer to a specific prayer we prayed. Many people think, *Well, this would have happened anyway.* We often take the blessings of our health for granted, instead of praising Him every day and giving thanks that He is our Healer.

We need to praise Jesus that He is our healer whether we are healed at that moment or not. We have to remember that God heals in His way and in His time. Though Jesus came to earth as our Healer, not all sickness or injury gets healed in this lifetime—at least not the way *we* always want it to be. If He doesn't heal us the way we ask Him to, it's because He has a greater plan and His glory will be seen in it.

Some sickness comes from the enemy. God allowed Job to be made sick by Satan. God allowed it for a reason. And even though we don't understand the reason that God doesn't always heal us, we can trust that He will bring good out of our suffering. If nothing else, suffering forces us to draw closer to Him. And the closer we are to Him, the more we will praise Him.

Praying passionately and fervently for our own healing is not a problem because we are never apathetic about that, in fact we feel quite strongly about it. And the sicker, the more miserable, pained, and incapacitated we are, the more fervently we pray. The Bible says that if we are suffering, we are to pray, and we are to pray with passion. That means burning, devout, sincere, and enthusiastic prayer. That means with our whole heart. When we pray for healing, we pray passionately, knowing that the answer is all up to God. He is our healer, but not all of us find the healing we want when we want it. Sometimes the healing is delayed and we can grow weary in the waiting. Time passes very slowly when we are in pain or are suffering.

In God's presence there is healing. When we praise God, it invites His presence into our lives in a powerful way. Praising God for His presence and healing power in the midst of our sickness, pain, weakness, or misery, opens up a channel through which His healing presence can penetrate our lives to heal us or to sustain us as He sees fit. That is the hidden power of praising God.

Heavenly Father, I thank You for all of the many blessings
You have bestowed upon my life. I praise You especially
as my healer and thank You for all the times You have
healed me in the past and will heal me in the future.
Thank You that even as I praise You now, Your healing
presence is penetrating my life and making me whole.
In Jesus' name I pray.

The ACT of CELEBRATION

"Speak to the Israelites and say to them: 'These are my appointed feasts, the appointed feasts of the LORD, which you are to proclaim as sacred assemblies'" (Leviticus 23:2).

In the Old Testament world, festivals marked the changing of the seasons, the bringing of the harvest, the shearing of the sheep, and so on. For the Israelite nation, these feast days were also spiritual markers of the journey the people had taken under God's care.

The most basic feast was the Sabbath, a day set aside every week to rest as God had in creation. Another frequent feast was the monthly new moon festival. This was a celebration of God's faithfulness to His people and to the covenant He had made with their ancestors.

Then there were the annual feasts. These celebrations commemorated significant historical events in which God had shown Himself in a mighty way. The Feast of Trumpets commemorated the giving of the Ten Commandments. The Passover was a reminder of the final plague by which God freed the people from Egypt. The Feast of Tabernacles memorialized the journey of the Israelites to their promised land.

Some of our holidays commemorate spiritual events as well: Easter, Christmas, Lent, and others. We use these holidays to join as communities of faith and remember together what God has done in us and among us.

We can each establish our own times of celebration. What has God done specifically in your life that might be cause for celebration? Part of the celebration of Old Testament feasts involved seeing old friends and returning to old places. Are there people with whom you can connect in order to encourage one another spiritually? Is there someone in your life who led you into a relationship with Jesus or who has had a special impact in your walk with God? Ask God to show you how to best celebrate those special events and show your appreciation to those involved. Praying for that person would be a great way to celebrate. Sending a note of thanks would be another. Invite God to help you build these kinds of living monuments that remind you of your journey with Him.

Dear God, I celebrate the moment when I came to know You as my Lord. I celebrate the times You have healed me and blessed me. I celebrate Your answers to my prayers and the times You saved me from my own mistakes. I celebrate the wonderful people You have put in my life—especially the ones who have led me closer to You and taught me to live Your way. I celebrate my life with You every day. In Jesus' name I pray.

DEVELOPING *a* HEART *for* WORSHIP

Read and Consider
Zechariah 7

"Ask all the people of the land and the priests, 'When you fasted and mourned in the fifth and seventh months for the past seventy years, was it really for me that you fasted?'" (Zechariah 7:5).

Zechariah had a message for his people—and it wasn't a pleasant one. He wanted them to understand that just worshiping, fasting, and keeping all the rituals of the faith was of no value. It meant nothing to God because it meant nothing to the people. They were not doing these acts out of love and devotion for God.

It's not enough that you should read about worship, hear worship songs, or listen to other people worship; you must actually worship God with a heart full of love for Him. It's in your own personal worship times that you will develop an intimate relationship with Him. If you are ever worshiping God by yourself and you don't sense His intimate presence, continue to praise and worship Him until you do. It's not that you have to try hard to get God to be close to you. He has chosen to dwell in your praise. But you do have to give Him time to break down the barriers in your soul and penetrate the walls of your heart so that He can pour Himself into you.

God must always be the complete focus of your worship. But when you worship Him, there will be gifts and blessings that He will pour out on you.

In worship you will sense why you were created. You will hear God speak to your heart because He has softened it and made it less resistant. In worship you will experience God's love. He will change your emotions, attitudes, and patterns of thought. He will pour out His Spirit upon you and make your heart open to receive all He has for you. He will give you clarity of mind so you can better understand His Word. He will refresh, renew, enrich, enlighten, heal, free, and fulfill you. He will breathe life into the dead areas of your existence. He will infuse you with His power and His joy. He will redeem and transform you and your situation. He will fill your empty places, liberate you from bondage, take away your fear and doubt, grow your faith, and give you peace. He will break the chains that imprison you and restore you to wholeness. He will lift you above your circumstances and limitations, and motivate you to help others find life in Him.

Dear Lord, help me to never get to the point where I take Your presence in my life lightly. Keep me from taking for granted the things I do for You so that they will not lose their life and meaning in my heart. I know my fasting, praying, and worshiping mean nothing to You if they mean nothing to me. Help me to do all things in a way that pleases You.
In Jesus' name I pray.

TEN GOOD REASONS *to* ASK GOD *for* WISDOM

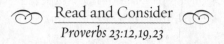

Read and Consider
Proverbs 23:12,19,23

"Buy the truth and do not sell it; get wisdom,
discipline and understanding" (Proverbs 23:23).

If you were given a choice between wealth and wisdom, which would you choose? The Bible never promises that financial gain will bring us increased happiness, but Scripture consistently teaches that we *should* ask for wisdom. Think of wisdom as the ability to exercise good judgment and discern correctly at all times. Wouldn't it be wonderful to have that ability? All we have to do is ask God for it! "Wisdom is supreme; therefore get wisdom. Though it cost all you have, get understanding" (Proverbs 4:7).

Here are ten good reasons to ask God for wisdom:

1. *To have longevity, blessings, and honor.* "Long life is in her right hand; in her left hand are riches and honor" (3:16).

2. *To live a good, peaceful life.* "Her ways are pleasant ways, and all her paths are peace" (3:17).

3. *To enjoy vitality and happiness.* "She is a tree of life to those who embrace her; those who lay hold of her will be blessed" (3:18).

4. *To be protected.* "Then you will go on your way in safety, and your foot will not stumble" (3:23).

5. *To experience refreshing rest.* "When you lie down, you will not be afraid; when you lie down, your sleep will be sweet" (3:24).

6. *To gain confidence.* "The LORD will be your confidence and will keep your foot from being snared" (3:26).

7. *To live in security.* "Do not forsake wisdom, and she will protect you; love her, and she will watch over you...When you walk, your steps will not be hampered; when you run, you will not stumble" (4:6,12).

8. *To be promoted.* "Esteem her, and she will exalt you; embrace her, and she will honor you" (4:8).

9. *To be saved from evil.* "For wisdom will enter your heart, and knowledge will be pleasant to your soul. Discretion will protect you, and understanding will guard you. Wisdom will save you from the ways of wicked men, from men whose words are perverse" (2:10-12).

10. *To be guided in the way you should go.* "Let the wise listen and add to their learning, and let the discerning get guidance" (1:5).

Ask God today to give you wisdom in all things.

Lord, I pray You would give me wisdom so that I will have a long life of peace, blessing, and happiness. Give me wisdom that brings confidence, protection, security, promotion, and guidance. I pray to have the kind of wisdom that saves me from evil and enables me to make right decisions. Along with all that, teach me to live with clear understanding, revelation, and truth. In Jesus' name I pray.

GETTING ARMED *for the* BATTLE

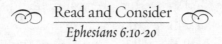
*"Put on the full armor of God so that you can take
your stand against the devil's schemes...Pray in the
Spirit on all occasions with all kinds of prayers and
requests. With this in mind, be alert and always keep
on praying for all the saints" (Ephesians 6:11,18).*

Scripture tells us that we are in a spiritual battle, and we need to be fully covered in the armor of God. From the moment we become believers and align ourselves with God and His purposes, the enemy of our soul wages war against us. Evil may be perpetrated against us by human beings, but we must never forget that it is our ultimate enemy, the devil, who is behind it. "For our struggle is not against flesh and blood, but against the rulers, against the authorities, against the powers of this dark world and against the spiritual forces of evil in the heavenly realms" (6:12).

God's Word, however, tells us how to protect ourselves. First, we are commanded to be strong in the Lord and in His power. Our own human strength is totally inadequate to do battle with our ultimate adversary, but God's power is invincible and His protection is complete.

The way we access that power and protection in this war that the enemy is waging against us is to put on God's armor. Paul tells us of the specific pieces of armor that each believer needs to consciously put on every day: the belt of truth (to fight Satan's lies), the breastplate of righteousness (to protect our hearts), shoes (for firm footing in our walk with Christ), the shield of faith (to repel Satan's accusations), the helmet of salvation (to protect our minds), and the sword of the Spirit—the Word of God (to give us knowledge, instruction, and ever-increasing faith).

Most of all, we must pray! Prayer strengthens us to stand against the enemy. Pray God's covering over yourself and your loved ones daily. Pray that He will reveal to you any place in your protective armor through which the evil one can secure a hook. Pray that any stronghold Satan is trying to erect in your life will be destroyed.

The enemy of our souls will always try to keep us from moving into all God has for us. But we can thwart his plans with prayer, praise, and the sword of the Spirit—which is the Word of God. These are our greatest weapons, and the devil cannot stand against them.

Lord, because I have aligned myself with You, the enemy wages war against me. Help me to put on the full spiritual armor You have provided for me. Teach me what each part of that is so I understand how to maintain and use it. Help me to fully understand the depth of truth, righteousness, faith, a solid walk with Christ, salvation, powerful prayer, and the sword of the Spirit, which is Your Word. In Jesus' name I pray.

PRAISE IS YOUR GREATEST WEAPON

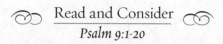

Read and Consider
Psalm 9:1-20

"I will praise you, O LORD, with all my heart; I will tell of all your wonders…For he who avenges blood remembers; he does not ignore the cry of the afflicted" (Psalm 9:1,12).

Have you noticed how many psalms either begin or end with praise? Praise is *not* denial. The Bible never tells us to bury our pain. Instead, we are to pour it out like water from a pitcher: "I pour out my complaint before him; before him I tell my trouble" (142:2). However, once we've expressed our distressing emotions to God, He gives us a powerful weapon with which we can fight our battles—the weapon of praise.

God wants us to *destroy* evil, not just try to outrun it. He doesn't want us to only try to defend ourselves and stay alive; He wants us to push the enemy back. He wants us to say as David did, "I pursued my enemies and crushed them; I did not turn back till they were destroyed. I crushed them completely, and they could not rise; they fell beneath my feet. You armed me with strength for battle; you made my adversaries bow at my feet" (2 Samuel 22:38-40).

Praise is one of our greatest weapons of warfare. "The weapons we fight with are not the weapons of the world. On the contrary, they have divine power to demolish strongholds" (2 Corinthians 10:4). When we praise God, our enemies have to turn back from attacking because they cannot stand in His presence. Every time you praise Jesus for His victory on the cross, it reminds the devil of his greatest defeat. And he hates that.

You don't have to praise God *for* your troubles, but you can praise

Him in the *midst* of them. And rest secure that He "remembers; he does not ignore the cry of the afflicted" (Psalm 9:12).

Thank You, God, that You never forget me. You always remember me and my situation, and You never ignore my cries to You when I am in need. I praise You in the middle of the struggles I face, knowing that worshiping You is my greatest weapon against the enemy of my soul. Help me to not just survive the attacks of the enemy, but to push the enemy back and resist him so he will flee from me. In Jesus' name I pray.

Look *to* God *as* Your Protector

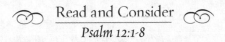
"'Because of the oppression of the weak and the groaning of the needy, I will now arise,' says the LORD. 'I will protect them from those who malign them'" (Psalm 12:5).

I know what it's like to have lived in the "bad part of town," where people are murdered, mugged, raped, and robbed. Where it wasn't safe to go out of the house. Fearing for my safety became a way of life there. In fact, many times I wondered if I would ever make it out of that place alive. No one stays in the bad part of town if they can possibly afford to live anywhere else.

After I came to know the Lord, I found the greatest comfort in being able to trust God as my Protector. God promises to rise up and protect the oppressed and needy from their oppressors. God did that for me. I intensely *yearned* for safety for years. He not only protected me in the dangerous place where I lived, but He led me to a place of safety.

We should never take for granted the protection of the Lord in our lives. We should not enter a plane, train, or automobile without praising Him as our Protector. We should not enter a day without *asking* Him for His protection and then thanking Him for it in advance. How many times have we been protected and spared from harm or disaster that we are not even aware of?

Remember, God also promises protection from those who malign you or who try to destroy your reputation without just cause. "It is mine to avenge; I will repay. In due time their foot will slip; their day of disaster is near and their doom rushes upon them" (Deuteronomy 32:35). He hears your prayerful groanings. He knows your needs.

When you are slandered or your life is threatened, rest assured that God promises divine protection. Your life is safe in His hands.

Lord, I am grateful for all the times You have protected me
from disaster. I'm sure there are countless ways You have
kept me from harm that I am not even aware of. I pray
You will always protect me and my reputation from anyone
who would try to destroy me. Thank You that You hear my
prayers for protection and You have promised to keep me safe.
In Jesus' name I pray.

PUTTING GOD ABOVE ALL ELSE

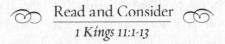

Read and Consider
1 Kings 11:1-13

*"As Solomon grew old, his wives turned his heart
after other gods, and his heart was not fully
devoted to the LORD his God, as the heart of
David his father had been" (1 Kings 11:4).*

With all God had given him, how could someone as wise as Solomon get so far off of the narrow path of obedience and so far away from the Lord's ways? Could it be that his wisdom turned out to be a point of pride? Did he think that *he* was the one responsible for all his wealth and blessings, and not God?

For half of his 40-year reign, Solomon seems to have exercised his wisdom in ways that pleased God. But little mention is made of Solomon's prayer life during these years. He presented sacrifices at the temple three times a year, but there is no record of his conversations with God during those visits. Perhaps the temple visits became merely a formality.

At the 20-year mark, cracks began to form in the structure of Solomon's reign. The first indication of a problem can be seen in the way he treated a friend (Hiram) by giving him a cheap gift (1 Kings 9:10-14). The queen of Sheba arrived and heaped praise on Solomon for his wisdom, though she was careful to give God the credit for Solomon's successes. Despite this foreign leader's enthusiastic words about the God of Israel, there's no hint in the passage that Solomon agreed with her or encouraged her interest in the God who had blessed his kingdom.

Solomon's reputation led to great riches. He accumulated things: ships, horses, gold, chariots, palaces, and women—lots of women.

He filled his life with treasures, and that's where his heart ended up. "King Solomon was greater in riches and wisdom than all the other kings of the earth" (10:23). God had promised this. After Solomon had asked for wisdom to rule the nation, God had responded, "I will give you what you have not asked for—both riches and honor—so that in your lifetime you will have no equal among kings" (3:13). With all that wisdom, the riches should not have gone to his head. But they did.

Jesus said, "Where your treasure is, there your heart will be also" (Matthew 6:21). Once Solomon's heart was focused on his material wealth, it was easy for his foreign wives to turn his heart away from the God who had so richly blessed him.

Any one of us can be tempted to put the things of this world above our relationship with God. That's why we have to regularly ask Him to show us if any of our possessions or desires are getting in the way of our walk with Him. We must ask the Lord not only for wisdom regarding that, but also for strength to resist anything that tempts our heart to turn away from Him.

God, I pray my treasure will always be in You and not in my possessions or the distractions of this world. Help me to never make an idol out of anything or anyone, or put them before You in any way. I give You honor and gratitude for all the good things You have given me. My greatest desire is for You, and I put You above all else in my life.
In Jesus' name I pray.

FINDING *a* NEW HEART

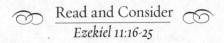

Read and Consider
Ezekiel 11:16-25

"I will give them an undivided heart and put a new spirit in them; I will remove from them their heart of stone and give them a heart of flesh" (Ezekiel 11:19).

There's an old hymn that contains these poignant words: "Prone to wander, Lord, I feel it; prone to leave the God I love." Many of us experience the temptation to wander spiritually—to drift away from the God we love. Our hearts and emotions can be desperately deceptive, convincing us all too easily that we want what someone else has and not what God has planned for us. "The heart is deceitful above all things and beyond cure. Who can understand it?" (Jeremiah 17:9).

There is One, however, who *does* understand how emotionally fragmented our hearts can become, and He has promised to give us an undivided heart. What does this mean? Simply this: God promises that when we relinquish control of our hearts to Him, He will transform us from the inside out. If you think you can't give up that destructive habit, those inappropriate thoughts, that illicit relationship, then seek God. Cry out for His help. Ask Him to give you an undivided heart. God specializes in spiritual surgery on hearts that are open to Him.

God also promises to remove our hearts of stone. Have you experienced such pain and trauma in your life that you have determined never to allow yourself to be that hurt again? Has your warm heart for the things of the Lord ever become cold and distant? When we invite God's Spirit to truly take up residence within us, He lights a fire in the hearth of our hearts that cannot be put out. Ask God today to ignite a fire within your heart so that it can burn away all hardness. Ask Him to give you a new heart filled with His love.

Dear God, I pray You will fill me with Your love, and help me to keep my heart from wandering away from You. Make my heart to be undivided and take away any hard-heartedness in me. I invite You to be in charge of my mind and emotions and enable me to surrender complete control to You. Light a flame of desire in me for You that never goes out. In Jesus' name I pray.

PRAYING GOD'S WORD

∽ <u>Read and Consider</u> ∽
Isaiah 55:1-13

"As the rain and the snow come down from heaven,
and do not return to it without watering the earth
and making it bud and flourish…so is my word that
goes out from my mouth: It will not return to me
empty, but will accomplish what I desire and achieve
the purpose for which I sent it" (Isaiah 55:10-11).

Sometimes we get discouraged when we pray fervently about a situation and get no response. We may even wonder if God hears us. But Isaiah 55 promises that God's Word, like the rain and snow, does what it needs to do wherever it goes. It accomplishes what God desires and achieves the purpose for which He sends it.

That means there is a power in praying God's Word. And we need to remember that, especially when we are in the midst of a battle. We can't see it in the quiet of our prayer time, but the words we raise to heaven are weapons of warfare. Because of our prayers, angels fight with demons to bring about God's will.

God's Word is "living and active. Sharper than any double-edged sword, it penetrates even to dividing soul and spirit, joints and marrow; it judges the thoughts and attitudes of the heart" (Hebrews 4:12). Paul placed the Word of God as part of every Christian's armor, saying that we must carry "the sword of the Spirit, which is the word of God" (Ephesians 6:17). In short, God's Word pierces everything it touches. It is *never* ineffectual.

That's why it is so important for you to not only pray, but to also read your Bible daily. Underline it, claim its promises, pray the words back to God. When you don't know what to pray, look up a psalm and read it aloud as your prayer. You can never be at a loss for words when it comes to prayer because God has given you everything you need. When you pray His words, you tap into His power and wield His sword. God promises that great things will happen when you do.

The battle for our lives, and the lives and souls of our children, our husbands, our friends, our families, our neighbors, and our nation is waged on our knees. When we don't pray, it's like sitting on the sidelines watching those we love and care about scrambling through a war zone, getting shot at from every angle. When we *do* pray, however, we're in the battle alongside them, appropriating God's power on their behalf. If we also declare the Word of God in our prayers, then we wield a powerful weapon against which no enemy can prevail.

Heavenly Father, I thank You that Your Word
always accomplishes the purpose for which You sent
it. Enable me to secure the power and life that is in
Your Word by having it planted so firmly in my heart
that it guides everything I do. Help me to weave Your
Word into my prayers so that it becomes a powerful
weapon against which the enemy cannot prevail.
In Jesus' name I pray.

The POWER of FASTING with PRAYER

ᘓᕲ Read and Consider ᕲᘓ
Ezra 8:21-32

*"So we fasted and petitioned our God about this,
and he answered our prayer" (Ezra 8:23).*

E zra the priest, and those traveling with him, needed protection for what would be a long and difficult journey. They could have asked the king for horses and soldiers, but they didn't. They could have hired guards, but they didn't. In fact, Ezra says he was ashamed to do that. After all, they had told the king how powerful their God was. Surely He could protect them on their way.

So they fasted and prayed.

Prayer is always a strong weapon against the enemy. Fasting makes it even more so. When the Lord puts on your heart that a particular request needs to be accompanied by fasting, you would be wise to listen. Fasting takes prayer to a whole new level, keeping evil at bay and breaking down strongholds. Fasting is a way of saying, "I deny myself what I want most and put God first in my life." The enemy hates that because he knows it's a sure way of resisting and defeating him. Fasting cripples the power of evil spiritual forces in the realm of darkness so they cannot sustain their grip on your life, your mind, and your circumstances.

Fasting and prayer bring your body into submission by informing it that it is not in charge. Fasting says, "I'm a spiritual being before I'm a physical being. I'm physical, so I need to eat, but I'm spiritual too. I'm going to assert the supremacy of my spiritual allegiance beyond and before my allegiance to my body and its desire for food."

Ezra was facing a difficult but very important trip, so he fasted and prayed. Whenever you are facing a difficult circumstance or decision, you can be sure that when you fast and pray about it, much is being accomplished in the spiritual realm. In fact, far more is accomplished in the realm of the spirit during a fast than is ever manifested immediately in the physical realm.

The kind of fast God wants is that of an obedient heart willing to say, "Yes, God, I'll go without food for a period if that means a child may be healed, a friend in bondage may be set free, a lost family member may be found, someone in darkness may be moved into light, or that I might live in greater wisdom, peace, and power. Yes, God, a fast is a small price to pay for all that."

Be open to hear what the Lord says to you about fasting, for He *is* saying something. If you are able to fast, He wants you to do so because you trust Him, love Him, and acknowledge His power.

Lord, help me to fast and pray regularly. Show me how often and how long and give me the strength to get through each fast successfully. With every fast, help me to pray powerfully about the issues of my life and the situations in my world. I want to deny my flesh so that I can exalt You above everything else in my life. In Jesus' name I pray.

APPROACH GOD'S THRONE
with CONFIDENCE

Read and Consider
Hebrews 4:14-16

"For we do not have a high priest who is unable to sympathize with our weaknesses, but we have one who has been tempted in every way, just as we are—yet was without sin. Let us then approach the throne of grace with confidence, so that we may receive mercy and find grace to help us in our time of need" (Hebrews 4:15-16).

Jesus understands us completely. That's because He left heaven and came to earth as a human being. He was "in very nature God, [but] did not consider equality with God something to be grasped, but made himself nothing, taking the very nature of a servant, being made in human likeness" (Philippians 2:6-7). He was fully God, yet a human being like us. He suffered heartache, persecution, pain, and suffering, so He is able to sympathize with *our* heartache, persecution, pain, and suffering. He was tempted in every way, so He understands *our* struggle with temptation. Though He never gave in to temptation, He understands that *we* often do.

That's why when we pray—especially in times of weakness, temptation, confusion, or shame—we must pray boldly and with confidence, knowing that Jesus understands us. Knowing that He is right there in the middle of whatever is troubling us, intervening on our behalf. Knowing that because we have aligned ourselves with Him—God's beloved Son who died to save us—God listens to our prayers as His beloved children. We can have confidence before God because of Jesus.

*Thank You, Jesus, that You understand my weaknesses
and my temptations, for You have been tempted in
every way and yet did not sin. Because You understand
my struggles, I know I can come to You and receive
mercy. Help me to approach You with the confidence
of knowing You will help me in my time of need.
In Jesus' name I pray.*

The POWER of FAITH

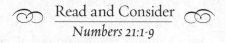

Read and Consider
Numbers 21:1-9

"The people came to Moses and said, 'We sinned when
we spoke against the LORD and against you. Pray that
the LORD will take the snakes away from us.' So Moses
prayed for the people. The LORD said to Moses, 'Make
a snake and put it up on a pole; anyone who is bitten
can look at it and live'" (Numbers 21:7-8).

When you read this passage, do you find yourself becoming frustrated with the stubborn ingratitude of the Israelites? In response to their plea, God had granted them victory over their enemies, the Canaanites. We don't know for certain how long the travels mentioned here lasted, but we do know that "the people grew impatient on the way; they spoke against God and against Moses" and were discontent with the food God provided for them.

Once again we're reminded of the vital importance of the confession of sin. Once again we witness the privilege of intercession, as Moses represented the Israelites' contrition before God. But this passage also bears witness to one of the most compelling principles in Scripture: The power of prayer is most clearly seen in the presence of faith.

Why would God give Moses such a seemingly strange command— to fashion an imitation snake out of bronze metal and put it up on a pole? What's more, God added this promise: Anyone who was bitten by a real snake could simply *look* at the bronze snake and live.

Of course, the artificial snake had no power, but Moses' obedience to the unusual instruction is recorded as well as the result that any person who followed God's command was saved. It was that simple, yet apparently some did not look at the snake. In their stubbornness and rebellion, many refused to believe that something so simple could save them.

It's still that way today. Jesus died on the cross to save us from the venom that infects us and leads to death—which is sin. Yet millions of people are wandering in the desert of their own sin because they refuse to lift their eyes to the cross. They refuse to believe that something so simple could save them.

The bronze snake on the pole is a type or picture of Jesus. Jesus even refers to this imagery in His conversation with Nicodemus recorded in John 3:14-15: "Just as Moses lifted up the snake in the desert, so the Son of Man must be lifted up, that everyone who believes in him may have eternal life." In both instances, it takes a willingness to look up and believe.

Christ is our mediator, and He loves us so much that He paid the penalty for our sin with His death. That means that those of us who look to Jesus as our Savior will live eternally with Him.

Lord Jesus, I look to You as my Savior and to what
You accomplished on the cross as the guarantee of my
salvation. Thank You for paying the price for my sin.
Forgive me if I have ever spoken against You in any
way, or have been motivated by fear and doubt. I come
to You in faith, believing that You hear me and will
answer my prayer. Help me to always live Your way.
In Jesus' name I pray.

REMAINING *in* HIM

John 15:1-11

"If you remain in me and my words remain in you, ask whatever you wish, and it will be given you" (John 15:7).

Eleven times the word *remain* is used in this short section. Eleven times Jesus chose this term to express the kind of relationship He wants us to have with Him. We are to remain in Christ. We are to remain in His love. If we do that, He will remain in us, His words will remain in us, and our lives will be fruitful.

So what does it mean to remain in Jesus? It means walking with Him and staying close and constantly plugged into Him, just like a branch remains with the vine. When a branch is part of the vine, it bears fruit. Conversely, when a branch is removed from the vine, it dies. Jesus says that if we remain in Him—spend time with Him, learn more about Him, get to know Him, be honest with Him, acknowledge our sins to Him—then we'll bear much fruit.

Jesus wants us to know His Word and allow it to become part of us. That means we need to be reading the Bible so that His words will be woven into the fabric of our being. We must know it so well that it becomes our guide, a source of renewal and knowledge of God's will. We must let it increase our understanding of who God is and who we are in Him.

God says if we remain in Him and let His words remain in us, we can ask of Him whatever we want and He will answer. That doesn't mean we will always get whatever we want. It means that because we are so closely entwined with Christ, we will have His mind and will learn how to pray for what He wants for our lives. When we do that, we end up doing His will and seeing answers to our prayers.

*Lord, help me to walk close to You every day and stay
constantly in communication with You—both by
talking to You and listening to You speak to my heart.
Help me to stay deeply in Your Word, learning more
about You and getting to know You better. Help me to
increase in the knowledge of Your ways and Your will.
In Jesus' name I pray.*

TIMING IS EVERYTHING

*"He has made everything beautiful in its time. He has also set
eternity in the hearts of men; yet they cannot fathom what
God has done from beginning to end" (Ecclesiastes 3:11).*

When it comes to prayer, most of us think about timing—that is, we think about what the timing of God's answers should be. *When the answer doesn't come immediately,* we anxiously wonder why. But Ecclesiastes tells us, "There is a time for everything, and a season for every activity under heaven." God's timing is not the same as ours. His ways are not our ways. We live our lives with a sense of earthly time. God sees things from an eternal perspective. Living in our time-bound world and waiting for God's timing is often hard, especially when we ask for things we want or need now.

We have to remember that even though we pray and have faith, the final outcome and timing are in *God's* hands. He says there is "a time to heal" (3:3). So if you pray for healing and nothing happens, don't beat yourself up or be mad at God. God sometimes uses physical ailments to get our attention so He can speak to us. He wants us to fervently turn to Him. So keep praying and don't give up hope.

The same is true when praying that God will save someone's life. We don't have the final say over anyone's hour of death. The Bible says there is "a time to die" (3:2), but we are not the ones who decide that. God does. And we must accept His decision. We can pray, but *He* determines the outcome. We have to allow Him to do that without resenting or getting angry at Him.

God's timing is perfect. And it is liberating when we surrender to it. There is great freedom in simply laying our concerns and desires before Him and then trusting Him for the outcome. What joy there is in looking for God's goodness to us in the midst of our times of waiting. While you may not be able to understand exactly what God is doing, you can trust that He is doing something. He has your best interests at heart. And He will make everything in your life beautiful in *His* perfect time.

Lord, I know Your timing is not the same as mine. I
want all the answers to my prayers right now. But
You want me to be patient and wait on You. I lay my
concerns before You and leave the outcome in Your
hands. Help me to rest in the knowledge that Your
timing is perfect, just as everything You do is perfect.
In Jesus' name I pray.

REMEMBER ME, LORD

*"Hezekiah turned his face to the wall and prayed
to the LORD, 'Remember, O LORD, how I have
walked before you faithfully and with wholehearted
devotion and have done what is good in your eyes.'
And Hezekiah wept bitterly" (2 Kings 20:2-3).*

The prophet Isaiah had informed Hezekiah that he was going to die. Perhaps you've faced a similar situation, whether from a potentially terminal illness, a near fatal accident, or an iffy report from a medical test. Whenever you face your own mortality, what do you do? Hezekiah prayed.

His prayer was a plea not to be forgotten by God. "Remember how I've served You, Lord. Remember the good things I have done."

When we find ourselves in desperate circumstances—especially in a life-and-death situation—we want to say, "Remember me, Lord. I love You and want to serve You longer." We know God doesn't owe us that. But we also know He is a God of mercy and grace. And we are asking for His grace to be extended to us now.

One of the things Hezekiah's prayer did was to clearly identify God as the source of his healing and deliverance. By turning to God with his whole heart, he was coming to the only One who could change his fate. God heard his prayer and the cry of his heart and not only healed him but gave him 15 more years to live and serve.

When you are in a difficult situation, cry out to God as the source of your healing and deliverance. Thank Him that He is a God of mercy and grace.

Lord, You are my Healer and Deliverer. In times of sickness, injury, or affliction, I pray You would remember me and heal me from anything that would threaten to diminish or end my life. Help me to be able to serve You longer and ever more effectively and not succumb to the plans of the enemy for my demise. Bless me with Your health and wholeness.
In Jesus' name I pray.

When You're Feeling Overwhelmed

⌒ Read and Consider ⌒
Numbers 11:10-17

*"I will come down and speak with you there, and I will
take of the Spirit that is on you and put the Spirit on them.
They will help you carry the burden of the people so that
you will not have to carry it alone" (Numbers 11:17).*

H ave you ever been asked to take on a job that you knew was
much too big or too difficult for you, possibly one that did
not involve any kind of tangible reward? Perhaps it's a volunteer
position at a church or in your community, or you may have even
found yourself in the position of raising someone else's child.

Overwhelming as the task might seem, it grows even more challenging when those you are serving don't seem to appreciate your
efforts. In return for sacrifice, you get selfishness; your efforts at
caretaking are met with complaining. At times like these you may
be tempted to cry out to the Lord as Moses did, "Why have you
brought this trouble on me? This burden is too heavy for me."

The Israelites were wallowing in the darkness of bitterness, casting
blame upon God and His chosen leader. Instead of choosing to
see God's hand in the moment, they blamed Moses and God for
everything that disappointed them. As a result, their suffering was
prolonged.

There is a crucial difference between the complaining that the
Israelites did in the desert and the complaints Moses expressed:
The people groused to one another, but Moses took his concerns to
the only One who could do something about them—God.

As a result of Moses' plea for help, God promised to send

additional leaders who would help Moses carry the burden of the needs of the people. Never hesitate to take your troubles to God when you are feeling overwhelmed; He has promised that you do not have to carry them alone.

God, I lift up to You the areas of my life that are
overwhelming and burdensome. I have not come to You
to complain, but rather to seek Your help. Where I have
tried to handle everything in my own strength instead
of depending on You, I ask Your forgiveness. I pray
You will take each burden of my heart and enable me
to rise above every challenging situation in my life.
In Jesus' name I pray.

GOD DELIVERS

"But when they cried out to the LORD, he raised up for them
a deliverer, Othniel son of Kenaz, Caleb's younger brother,
who saved them…Again the Israelites cried out to the
LORD, and he gave them a deliverer—Ehud, a left-handed
man, the son of Gera the Benjamite" (Judges 3:9,15).

The Israelites' sinful ways put them into a place of bondage to foreign nations and foreign gods. But every time they cried out to the Lord, He was faithful to rescue them.

We all need deliverance at one time or another. That's because regardless of how spiritual we may be, we're still made of flesh. And no matter how good we may think we are, we have an enemy who is trying to erect strongholds of evil in our lives. Jesus taught us to pray, "Deliver us from the evil one" (Matthew 6:13). He would not have instructed us in that manner if we didn't need to be delivered. But so often we don't pray that way. So often we live our lives as if we don't realize Jesus paid an enormous price so we could be free. God wants to free us from everything that binds, holds, or separates us from Him. He wants to *continue* to set us free every day of our lives.

Do you feel enslaved to finances, illness, addictions, unhealthy relationships, immorality, or resentments? Do you struggle to be close to God or to believe that He hears your prayers and will answer them? Do you fear that you will never have victory over the areas you struggle with, and so you are more discouraged than joyful? God wants to set you free. He wants you to remember that He is the Deliverer. He says, "Call upon me in the day of trouble; I will deliver you, and you will honor me" (Psalm 50:15).

Deliverance is found by praying for it yourself (Psalm 72:12), by having someone else who is a strong believer pray with you for it (Psalm 34:17), by reading the truth of God's Word with great understanding and clarity (John 8:32), and by spending time in the Lord's presence. The most effective and powerful way to spend time in the Lord's presence is in praise and worship. Every time you worship God, something happens to break the power of evil. That's because God inhabits your praises, and this means you are in His presence.

Remember that deliverance is an ongoing process. God wants you whole and will see that process through to the end. Don't give up. "He who began a good work in you will carry it on to completion until the day of Christ Jesus" (Philippians 1:6).

Dear Lord, I pray that wherever the enemy has erected a stronghold in my life for my destruction, You would deliver me from it. Thank You that You paid the price for my freedom and You continue to set me free from the enemy's plans every day. I lift You up, exalt You, and praise You as my Savior and Deliverer. I am grateful that Your presence is welcomed by my praise. In Jesus' name I pray.

RESPONDING *to* GOD'S LOVE

*"For God so loved the world that he gave his one
and only Son, that whoever believes in him shall
not perish but have eternal life" (John 3:16).*

God loved us so much that He gave us His Son. Jesus loved us so much that He gave us His life. He did that so we could always be close to God and live with Him for eternity. He did that so we don't ever have to be separated from God. He did it so we could find healing and wholeness for our body, soul, and spirit. That's true love.

Jesus told Nicodemus the Old Testament story about the ancient Israelites wandering in the desert constantly complaining. As a punishment for their complaining, God sent snakes into the camp. But He also made a provision for those who would trust in Him. "The LORD said to Moses, 'Make a snake and put it up on a pole; anyone who is bitten can look at it and live'" (Numbers 21:8). Jesus was making an analogy referring to His imminent death on the cross. "The Son of Man must be lifted up, that everyone who believes in him may have eternal life" (John 3:14-15).

Jesus died to save us not because we earned it, or we were good enough, or deserved it because of how tough our lives are, but because He loves us. Jesus did so much for us, yet all He asks in return is that we look to Him and lift Him up in our hearts and with our words.

God loves the whole world. He loves you and me. That kind of love requires a response. That kind of love is an amazing invitation that we must accept or in some way reject. Rejecting God's love can take many forms; accepting His love takes only one—believing in His Son, Jesus.

All we have to do to respond to God's great love for us is say, "Jesus, I believe You died on the cross for me in order to give me forgiveness for my sins and eternal life with You. I receive that gift of salvation and redemption today and every day. I will respond to Your great love by lifting You up in praise continually, and loving You with all my heart forever."

Lord Jesus, it is hard to comprehend love so great as Yours. You laid down Your life for me so that I can live forever with You. I ask You to help me to lay down my life fully for You in serving Your purpose here on earth. My response to Your first loving me is to love You wholeheartedly in return. Help me to do that. In Jesus' name I pray.

How *to* Respond *to* Unanswered Prayer

∾∾ Read and Consider ∾∾
Isaiah 54:1-8

"'Sing, O barren woman, you who never bore a child;
burst into song, shout for joy, you who were never in labor;
because more are the children of the desolate woman than
of her who has a husband,' says the LORD*" (Isaiah 54:1).*

When the prophet Isaiah foretold of Jerusalem's coming restoration, he likened its condition to a barren woman. He told the Israelites to sing in the face of it. This is exactly how we should respond to unanswered prayer or to the barren or unfruitful situations in our own lives. We are to sing praise to the One who can bring to life the places in us and our situations that appear to be dead. The One who can birth something new in us and our circumstances. The One who hears our prayers and answers in His way and His time. Whenever you have a dream in your life that seems to go unfulfilled year after year and there is no way possible to make it happen, determine to worship God in the face of it. When hope that this thing can ever be brought to life completely dies, then praise God for His resurrection power. The Bible tells us that not only can God bring to life things that are dead, but we are actually to prepare for that possibility because of who He is and what He does.

Have you ever experienced times when you are praying fervently from your whole heart and yet it seems that heaven and earth are silent? Do you ever wonder if God has even heard your prayers? If so, you are not alone. We've all felt that at times. But be assured that God hears and will answer. He may fall silent for a time, but His silence does not mean that He has not heard or that He has forgotten your request. What God has promised, He will perform. And when He does, you will be amazed that the answer is far beyond what you could have imagined. Until that time, sing praise to the Lord and see things come to life that you thought never would.

Lord, Your Word says to sing praise in the face of unfruitful
situations in our lives. So even when my prayers seem
to be unanswered I will still praise You, because I know
that You can breathe life into any situation—even one
that appears dead. Help me to always trust that You have
heard my prayers and have not forgotten my request.
In Jesus' name I pray.

Bringing Dead Things *to* Life

⟐ Read and Consider ⟐
Ezekiel 37:1-14

"This is what the Sovereign LORD says to these
bones: I will make breath enter you, and
you will come to life" (Ezekiel 37:5).

One of the most amazing things that God has placed within nature is its ability to re-create itself. Who doesn't rejoice at seeing flowers pop up from the ground, or leaves and blossoms budding on trees after a long winter when everything appeared lifeless and dead?

On the spiritual level as well, God specializes in bringing life where things might have seemed dead. This powerful story in Ezekiel is actually a metaphor—a word picture—of God's ability to restore life in seemingly hopeless situations. With God's hand upon him and led by His Spirit, the prophet Ezekiel sees a vision of an entire valley full of dry bones. God asks Ezekiel whether he thinks these bones can live. The prophet answers wisely: "You alone know" (37:3), and God proceeds to cover the bones with tendons, flesh, and skin. Then God gives Ezekiel the order to use His holy name to command the breath of life to enter the bones. To Ezekiel's amazement, a great army rises to its feet.

Just as this vision was a symbolic representation of God's intention to restore the nation of Israel after its years of captivity, it has also come to signify His ability to breathe new life into any seemingly hopeless situation. Have you ever used the word "dead" in connection with your life? Has the life gone out of your marriage? Does the church you attend seem lifeless and dull? Is your own heart for God without vibrancy? Does your work feel like it's sucking the life out of you? Just as God commanded Ezekiel to take action in His power, He has given us the power of prayer.

If your marriage lacks love, pray! If your church is without vitality, pray! If your walk with God is dry, pray! If your work is killing you slowly, pray! God is waiting to work through you to bring His life into places and situations you thought were dead. If dry bones can become a vast army, your situation is not beyond hope. You can see dead things brought to life through prayer.

Dear God, there are areas of my life that seem dead to me and they need a new infusion of Your life. There are dreams I have had that appear to have died because it's been a long time and still they have not been realized. I know if You can make dry bones into a vast army, You can bring life to anything worth praying about, no matter how dead it seems. In Jesus' name I pray.

Praise Is *the* Prayer That Changes Everything

"Hear my prayer, O LORD; let my cry for help
come to you. Do not hide your face from me when
I am in distress. Turn your ear to me; when I
call, answer me quickly" (Psalm 102:1-2).

Once when I was enduring tremendous physical suffering, I randomly opened my Bible for comfort. Instead of turning to where the ribbon marked my place of ongoing reading, I found myself at Psalm 102. What I read there was written thousands of years ago, yet it could have been written for me right then in terms of what I was experiencing. The writer was honest before God about the way he was feeling and all that he was suffering, and he cried out to God to hear his prayer and give him a future. After reading the psalm, I did the same thing. Like the writer, I recognized that God will exist forever and will never change, and I have an eternal future with Him. No matter how bad it is here, I have the hope that whether God chooses to heal me or not, I have a life forever with Him that is free of pain, and I praise Him for that.

I have found that no matter how bad I feel, when I praise God I always feel better. I have found great healing in worship services where many people are worshiping God together. I have also found healing when worshiping God by myself. Things happen when we worship Him because praising God is the prayer that changes everything.

If you need to see a change in your life, your health, your circumstances, your financial situation, your attitude, your spouse, your children, or your church, then praise God! Thank Him for all that He can and will do—and invite Him to do it in His way and in His time. The Lord "will respond to the prayer of the destitute; he will not despise their plea" (Psalm 102:17). And His answers will be far better than anything you could have thought up for yourself!

Dear God, I worship You and thank You that You are greater than anything I face. Thank You that You are a compassionate God of mercy and You hear my prayers and answer them. I thank You that You inhabit my praise, and that in Your presence my life and circumstances are changed. I am grateful that praising You changes me. In Jesus' name I pray.

PRAISE GOD *for* HIS GREATNESS

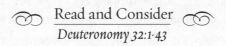

Read and Consider
Deuteronomy 32:1-43

"I will proclaim the name of the LORD. Oh, praise the greatness of our God! He is the Rock, his works are perfect, and all his ways are just. A faithful God who does no wrong, upright and just is he" (Deuteronomy 32:3-4).

Nothing we do is more powerful or life changing than praising God. It is one of the means by which God transforms us. Every time we praise and worship Him, His presence changes our hearts and allows the Holy Spirit to soften and mold us into whatever He wants us to be.

Because our flesh does not naturally praise and worship God, we have to *will* ourselves to do it. And because it's not the first thing we think to do, we have to decide to do it regardless of our circumstances. We have to say, "I *will* praise the Lord." Of course, the more we get to know God, the easier praise becomes. When we get to the point where we can't keep from praising Him, then we are at the place we are supposed to be.

Pause many times a day to praise God for the many blessings He's given you. Praise Him that He is your Rock, that His works are perfect, that His ways are just. Praise Him that He is a faithful and good God. Praise Him for how much He loves you and for all the ways He shows it.

Do you want a transformed life? Do you want to be more like Jesus? Do you want to be molded into all that God wants you to be? Then praise Him often. When you think of all He has done for you, praise and worship will come easily.

God, I praise You for Your greatness and goodness. I worship You as the God of creation and the Lord of my life. I praise You in the good times and in the difficult times as well. Thank You that You show Your love for me by protecting me, providing for me, delivering me, and giving me Your peace and power. In Jesus' name I pray.

SEEING GOD *in the* DARK

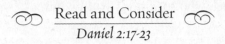
"During the night the mystery was revealed to Daniel in a vision. Then Daniel praised the God of heaven and said: 'Praise be to the name of God for ever and ever; wisdom and power are his'" (Daniel 2:19-20).

Why is it that during the daylight hours when we're active and busy, our problems don't seem as serious? But when darkness falls and the lights go out, our fears and worries loom larger. Perhaps it's because we forget that we serve a God who never sleeps and is sovereign over our affairs both day and night. The sovereignty of God is a major theme of the book of Daniel. Throughout this book we see multiple reasons that Daniel and his friends had to praise God for His power and ultimate authority over the situations that literally kept them up at night.

Are you facing situations that cause you to lose sleep at night? If so, you're not alone. For centuries God's people have experienced what are sometimes called "dark nights of the soul." Take comfort in the fact that God uses these times of darkness to teach us invaluable lessons we might never learn in the light. He desires to teach us things about Himself that we will only learn in the dark—when we are holding tightly to Him and He has our undivided attention. During those times, we will be the losers if we resist Him and what He is trying to teach us. He wants to share His secrets with us. "He reveals deep and hidden things; he knows what lies in darkness, and light dwells with him" (2:22).

One of the biggest mistakes we can make is to be angry with God because of things that happen. Or don't happen. "Woe to him who quarrels with his Maker" (Isaiah 45:9). Instead, allow God to use these dark times to give you "the treasures of darkness, riches stored in secret places, so that you may know that I am the LORD, the God of Israel, who summons you by name" (Isaiah 45:3).

Lord, it seems that in the middle of the night all
problems appear larger. At those times I am reminded
that You never sleep, and I can come to You and cling
to Your presence. I pray that at those times You will
give me the treasures of darkness, stored in secret places,
as You have spoken of in Your Word. I pray You will
fill my darkness with Your light and give me peace.
In Jesus' name I pray.

PERSEVERING PRAYER

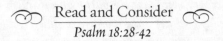

Read and Consider
Psalm 18:28-42

"You armed me with strength for battle; you made my adversaries bow at my feet" (Psalm 18:39).

Perseverance has been described as the ability to see a problem or a situation through to its resolution despite the difficulties encountered on the way. It's not hard to persevere when everything's going your way, but when the road to resolution becomes a virtual obstacle course, we need the strength to persevere through the pressure.

God's Word tells us over and over again that perseverance, while it may not be fun, is actually good for us, "because we know that suffering produces perseverance; perseverance, character; and character, hope" (Romans 5:3-4). In fact, we are actually *commanded* to stay with the course God puts us on. "Run with perseverance the race marked out for us" (Hebrews 12:1).

Ask the Lord to help you do as David did and be aggressive against the enemy, who would try to wear you down with discouragement. Ask Him to help you stand strong against this enemy until he is completely destroyed. David didn't stop until the job was done, and neither should we. We should pray through until we see the answer.

Ask God to give you the strength you need in order to persevere in prayer. With His power flowing through you, you can not only withstand whatever pressures are coming your way, you can eliminate them. Remember, you don't run this obstacle course alone. God is with you and will arm you with strength for the battle. Because of that you will have the victory.

Lord, I am grateful that You have armed me with the strength I need for the battle ahead. Help me to subdue my enemies until they are completely destroyed. Teach me to persevere in prayer and not let down. Enable me to pray through each situation until I see victory over all opposition. Thank You that You are always with me, working things out in my favor.
In Jesus' name I pray.

PRAYER RISES

Revelation 8:1-5

*"The smoke of the incense, together with the
prayers of the saints, went up before God from
the angel's hand" (Revelation 8:4).*

You've watched smoke rise from a lighted candle or from the
chimney of a fireplace. It naturally goes up and disappears
beyond sight. In his wonderful vision of heaven, John saw an angel
carrying incense and the prayers of the saints. The aroma and smoke
rising up from the angel's hand were offerings to God.

In the Old Testament, the incense that burned on the altar was
also symbolic of prayers offered to God by the high priest: God
directed the Israelites to place the altar for burning incense "in front
of the curtain that is before the ark of the Testimony...where I will
meet with you. Aaron must burn fragrant incense on the altar every
morning when he tends the lamps. He must burn incense again when
he lights the lamps at twilight so incense will burn regularly before
the LORD for the generations to come" (Exodus 30:6-8).

This continued into the New Testament worship at the temple.
Luke 1 describes the priest Zechariah (the father of John the Baptist)
being chosen by lot to "go into the temple of the Lord and burn
incense." Incense continued to be burned twice daily at the temple.
And when the people saw the smoke rising, they prayed. Both the
smoke and their prayers ascended to God's throne.

This is a particularly encouraging picture for us on those days
when we feel as if our prayers don't have power enough to make it
past the ceiling. As if they just hang there in space or evaporate into
thin air. Or worse yet, as if they never even make it off the ground.

At those times, it's wonderful to know that the distance our prayers travel does not depend on the fervency of our prayers or how loud or well we say them. Just as smoke rises, so do our prayers rise to heaven and to the ears of God, because that's what prayers born of faith do.

Lord, how grateful I am that my prayers always rise
to You in heaven and You hear each one. Even the
quietest prayers of my heart born out of faith are as
important as my loudest prayers ignited by fervency.
Thank You that You will hear and answer them all.
How blessed am I to have You as the center of my life.
In Jesus' name I pray.

GOD HEARS *the* PRAYERS *of the* RIGHTEOUS

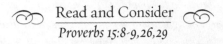

Read and Consider

Proverbs 15:8-9,26,29

"The LORD detests the sacrifice of the wicked, but the prayer of the upright pleases him" (Proverbs 15:8).

Certain principles in Scripture are repeated over and over again. Consider this chapter of Proverbs. Again and again we are reminded that "the LORD detests the way of the wicked but he loves those who pursue righteousness...The Lord detests the thoughts of the wicked, but those of the pure are pleasing to him" (15:9,26). Why the continual repetition of the importance of righteousness?

First, we need to remember what righteousness is *not:* It is not simply doing "good works." Scripture does not teach that we will obtain righteousness through our own efforts. Rather, we *become* righteous through our relationship with Jesus Christ. This is spelled out for us in the New Testament: "But now a righteousness from God, apart from law, has been made known...This righteousness from God comes through faith in Jesus Christ to all who believe" (Romans 3:21-22).

Any righteousness imparted to us, then, is due to our faith in Christ. Yet once we receive Christ as our Savior, God expects us to live as redeemed people—individuals who are characterized by spirits of humility, repentance, and submission to God's will in our lives. "What does the LORD require of you? To act justly and to love mercy and to walk humbly with your God" (Micah 6:8). Living according to His commandments and all the teaching found in His Word is righteous living. And we are promised that God will hear our prayers when we live His way.

Dear God, how grateful I am that You see me as righteous
because I have received Jesus as my Lord. But I know You
also want me to choose to live righteously as well.
I pray my thoughts, words, and actions will always be
pleasing in Your sight so that my prayers will be pleasing
to Your ears. Enable me every day to do what's right.
In Jesus' name I pray.

Prayers *of* Intercession

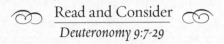
*"I feared the anger and wrath of the LORD, for he was
angry enough with you to destroy you. But again
the LORD listened to me. And the LORD was angry
enough with Aaron to destroy him, but at that time
I prayed for Aaron too" (Deuteronomy 9:19-20).*

When we step in on behalf of others in prayer, amazing things
can happen. This is proven over and over again throughout
Scripture, and the example in these verses is one of the most powerful
in the Bible. In this passage, Moses recounts to the new generation
of Israelites the story recorded in Exodus 32.

Picture the scene: Moses was away, meeting with the Lord to
receive instruction and guidance for the Israelites from their true
and faithful God. During Moses' long absence on the mountain,
however, the Israelites grew restless and impatient. They decided that
they needed an idol—a golden calf—to worship. And Aaron went
along with the plan. God's wrath was stirred toward the people, and
in spite of his own anger toward them, Moses intervened on their
behalf to prevent God from destroying them. And since Aaron had
succumbed to the people's demands and fashioned the idol, he was
ultimately responsible. Yet Moses interceded for his brother as well.

Our intercessions for others may be far less dramatic than this
example, but the extreme nature of this situation shows how powerful our prayers can be. We may be praying for another's healing,
encouragement, guidance, salvation, protection, or strengthening.
The Lord's response to Moses reveals that He listens to us and that
our prayers matter to Him. We can make a powerful impact on the

lives of those around us through our intercessions for them. Take the time to pray diligently for those whom the Spirit puts on your heart. Then watch what God does in their lives.

*God, help me to be one of Your faithful and powerful
intercessors. Help me to not be so focused on myself and my
situation that I don't see how to pray for the needs of others.
Give me strong faith to believe that my prayers can make a
big difference in their lives. Show me the people I need to
pray for today and how I should specifically pray for them.
In Jesus' name I pray.*

Our God-Given Authority

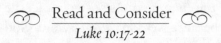

Read and Consider

Luke 10:17-22

*"I have given you authority to trample on snakes
and scorpions and to overcome all the power of the
enemy; nothing will harm you" (Luke 10:19).*

What does it mean that we have authority to overcome all the power of the enemy? Why did Jesus think it was so important to tell us this? Because our enemy is powerful, and he is working every day to hurt us, destroy us, and make us ineffective for God.

If we don't take our enemy seriously, it is much easier for Satan to manipulate and deceive us. We are all involved in a spiritual battle with an enemy who won't let up. Even though it is people who do evil things to us, we have to keep in mind that it is our ultimate enemy, the devil, who is behind it. "For our struggle is not against flesh and blood, but against the rulers, against the authorities, against the powers of this dark world and against the spiritual forces of evil in the heavenly realms" (Ephesians 6:12). Even when we are being attacked by a person, recognizing who our real enemy is will be the first step in standing strong.

The second step has to do with acknowledging the authority that has been given to us by Christ Himself. Our enemy is not as powerful as he wants us to believe. Satan is not even close to being as powerful as God is, but he wants us to think he is. And he will overpower anyone who doesn't understand that. Because of what Jesus accomplished on the cross, the devil is a defeated foe. He can't take our life and do what he wants with it unless we allow him to. He can't have our soul unless we give it to him. He can only accomplish what he does through lies and deception. It's our responsibility to recognize his lies and expose them for what they are. We do that by standing on the ultimate truth, which is the Word of God. The Word of God says that we have been given authority "to overcome all the power of the enemy." But so often we let the enemy get away with too much because we don't exercise our God-given authority to control his access to our lives.

When we face difficulty or oppression, we never need to live under the assumption that it's "just our bad luck." Instead, we can go before God in prayer, asking Him for discernment, wisdom, and strength to exercise the authority He has given us. Then we can get up and walk through our day as children of the King with all the honors, privileges, and authority of rightful heirs.

Dear God, help me to fully understand the authority You have given me over the enemy of my soul. Thank You, Jesus, that because of what You accomplished on the cross, the enemy is defeated. Enable me to always recognize his lies and deception and be able to stand strong on the truth of Your Word so that I can eliminate his access to my life.
In Jesus' name I pray.

PAYING ATTENTION *to* GOD'S DIRECTION

*"Zedekiah son of Josiah was made king of Judah
by Nebuchadnezzar king of Babylon; he reigned
in place of Jehoiachin son of Jehoiakim. Neither he
nor his attendants nor the people of the land paid
any attention to the words the LORD had spoken
through Jeremiah the prophet" (Jeremiah 37:1-2).*

This passage in Jeremiah reads like a script for a movie. Danger, courage, betrayal, drama, war, and political intrigue abound. Tensions stay at a fever pitch in a large city under siege. Our hero Jeremiah may not live to see another day. Special forces led by Ebed-Melech the Cushite have to pull off a daring rescue. Outside the walls, the mighty Chaldeans are waiting for the city to collapse. When and how will Jerusalem fall? Will God actually let that happen? When the end comes, who will be left standing? And why isn't anyone listening to the one prophet who is speaking for God? He's the good guy.

We can see it so clearly. Why can't they?

We can see things in that Old Testament scene because we have perspective and access to other information. But when you're in the middle of a situation, things aren't always so clear. As our life stories unfold, sometimes it's obvious who to listen to and who *not* to listen to; sometimes it's not. Sometimes we pay attention; sometimes we don't. The Director of our life movie is giving just enough information to bring us along on the right path. There may be surprises in the plot along the way—but He is not surprised. It's all part of the story. He gives directions and guidance, telling us where to go and what to do so that the story falls into place as it should. We just have to pay attention.

King Zedekiah kept asking Jeremiah for God's counsel, but then when he received God's directions, he didn't act on them. The king *wanted* to know, but he was unwilling to do anything with that knowledge. How often do we plead for God's direction and, not liking what we hear, decide to go our own way? We hear from God but then, for one reason or another, we don't immediately act on it.

When you are asking God for direction, ask Him to give you ears to hear it and the will and strength to follow it. Say, "God, show me what to do and enable me to do it."

*Father God, I ask You for clear direction in my life. Help
me to always hear and understand what it is You want me
to do. I don't want to miss Your instructions to my heart
because I did not listen. Enable me to act immediately
on the guidance You give me and not ignore it. Show
me what Your will is and enable me to accomplish it.
In Jesus' name I pray.*

WHEN WORDS DON'T COME

*"In the same way, the Spirit helps us in our weakness. We
do not know what we ought to pray for, but the Spirit
himself intercedes for us with groans that words cannot
express. And he who searches our hearts knows the mind
of the Spirit, because the Spirit intercedes for the saints
in accordance with God's will" (Romans 8:26-27).*

When we pray, we are talking to God—maybe out loud, or in
a whisper, or silently. Probably most of us try to carefully
choose the words we say. We want to get it just right, to be specific,
to talk to God in a way that is pleasing to Him and that really
expresses our hearts. But sometimes the words won't come. Sometimes the pain is too deep, the questions too difficult, the situation
too confusing or complex, the fear too acute. We want to talk to
God, but we don't know how to express what we feel. What then?

God promises that when we don't have the words, the Holy Spirit
prays *for* us! He searches our hearts and knows what's going on, and
He intercedes. He pleads with God on our behalf.

In times of grief or suffering—when we can barely see past the
pain to communicate with anyone…the Holy Spirit helps us to pray.

In times of uncertainty—when we are so unsure of the path
ahead that we don't even know what kind of guidance to ask for…
the Holy Spirit helps us to pray.

In times of fear—when we are so frightened that we don't know
where to turn or whom to trust…the Holy Spirit helps us to pray.

In times of feeling overwhelmed—when the crushing weight
on our shoulders pushes us to our knees…the Holy Spirit helps us
to pray.

When you can't find the words, simply sit with God and invite the Holy Spirit to enable you to communicate to God your deepest thoughts, feelings, fears, and doubts. He will help you pray.

Lord, I don't know how to pray about certain things, but You do. Holy Spirit, help me in my weakness by interceding for me and through me. You know the will of the Father and You know what to pray. Guide me and teach me, especially when I have exhausted all words. Help me, Lord, to communicate my deepest thoughts, feelings, fears, and doubts, so that my prayers are pleasing to You. In Jesus' name I pray.

Praising God *for the* Future

*"Let us rejoice and be glad and give him glory! For
the wedding of the Lamb has come, and his bride
has made herself ready" (Revelation 19:7).*

We need to praise God for who He *is*. We must praise God
for what He has *done*. We should also praise God for what
He's *going* to do. The book of Revelation paints a picture of a future
world. A world put right side up. It describes a wedding feast to
which we are invited, a feast that inaugurates a new world where
sadness and fear have no place.

Praising God for what we know is coming doesn't mean that we
don't live fully in this day and in this moment. Instead, it means
that part of the sweetness of this moment is the anticipation of the
moments to come. In fact, knowing what is ahead allows us to better
savor what we have, to endure the difficulties, and to continue on
with courage.

Most often we praise God for the good things in our lives and
the ways He has provided for us. This is right to do. But along with
that, let's not forget to praise God that He will one day redeem this
world in every possible way. Let's thank Him ahead of time for the
feast that He will lay out before us—His beloved children—on
the day when He brings all of history to a close and eternity with
Him begins.

Let us rejoice in prayer right now that the wedding of the Lamb
is coming, and we, as His bride, are being made ready to be with
Him. Let us praise Him that our future is secure and good. Let's

worship Him now and thank Him that we are going to have the privilege of worshiping Him in heaven forever.

Lord God, I praise You for my future, for You have promised that it is good. Thank You that my ultimate end is with You in heaven. I praise You for redeeming everything in my life. As I worship You now, I thank You that one day I will have the great privilege of worshipping You face-to-face for all eternity. Until that time I will worship You every day of my life on earth. In Jesus' name I pray.

POWERFUL LISTENING

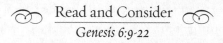

*"Noah was a righteous man, blameless among the people
of his time, and he walked with God" (Genesis 6:9).*

Noah listened well. When God spoke to him, he paid attention. Genesis tells us that Noah "walked with God." What a beautiful way to say that Noah lived each day with an awareness of God's presence. Beyond that, however, Noah also obeyed. What God told him to do, he did.

Noah obeyed even though God directed him to do something outlandish: "Make yourself an ark" (6:14). And Noah did. What a monstrosity he constructed on dry land, miles from the nearest body of water! How many insults, jokes, and sarcastic questions he must have endured. Yet he kept on task, obeying God's instructions. Hebrews 11:7 lists Noah among the heroes of faith. The picture that develops out of the phrase "walked with God" reveals a person who depended on God's faithfulness across the decades, through times of doubt, against the corruption that surrounded him.

With the exception of his family, Noah stood alone for God in his culture. The memory of God in the world had shrunk to a single man and his household. Many centuries later, Jesus described the people in Noah's day: "For in the days before the flood, people were eating and drinking, marrying and giving in marriage, up to the day Noah entered the ark; and they knew nothing about what would happen until the flood came and took them all away. That is how it will be at the coming of the Son of Man" (Matthew 24:38-39). In Noah's day, as in ours, the noises of busyness can drown out the voice of God. (Little did they know that a different kind of drowning would soon overtake them.) Jesus warned about any time when people are oblivious to the danger of going about life without stopping long enough to listen to God.

Prayer is more than talking to God. While that is vital, too many of us give God our list of requests and then dash off to our next task. What would our lives be like if we took the time not only to talk to God but to listen to Him as well? What if we then determined to obey what He tells us to do—no matter how much our society might scoff at us?

Do you want to walk with God? Then in your prayer time, *listen* carefully for His voice. You may hear Him leading you in a new direction, with a new purpose, and with courage you never knew you had!

Dear God, help me to live each day with a deep sense
of Your presence. I don't want to go through life without
taking time to be completely with You. I want my
relationship with You to be so strong that other people
recognize Your Spirit in me. Whenever I draw near
to You in prayer, help me to hear Your voice speaking
to my heart so that I will always follow Your leading.
In Jesus' name I pray.

FINDING *a* SONG *in the* NIGHT

Read and Consider
Job 35:1-16

*"But no one says, 'Where is God my Maker, who
gives songs in the night?'" (Job 35:10).*

O f all Job's friends, only Elihu had a glimmer of wisdom. In
fact, God rebukes the other three men for their inaccurate
explanations of Job's pain (42:7-9). Elihu wasn't completely in tune
with the sovereignty of God, but he understood that something good
would come from Job's pain. He observed that people often cry out
to God for deliverance, but rarely cry out for God Himself (35:10).

King David experienced suffering, and God gave him a song:

> *I waited patiently for the LORD; he turned to me and
>   heard my cry.*
> *He lifted me out of the slimy pit, out of the mud and mire;
>   he set my feet on a rock and gave me a firm place to stand.*
> *He put a new song in my mouth, a hymn of praise to our
>   God.*
> *Many will see and fear and put their trust in the LORD
>   (Psalm 40:1-3).*

In your darkest time, when you seek God, He will give you a
song in the night. It will be a song of worship and praise, and your
heart will sing once more. It doesn't matter how terrible or difficult
your situation is. Every time you praise God, He will move into the
situation to redeem and transform it in some way. Praise God for
how He will work through your pain, for the lives He will touch
through your witness. You may never know how far-reaching your

testimony will be, but rest assured that God will use you to glorify Him and to draw others closer to Jesus.

Lord, Your Word says that even in our darkest times, You
will give us a song in the night. When I am going through
a dark night of the soul, I pray You would enlighten my
darkness with a song that is music to my heart. In the face
of the darkest situation in my life, help me to lift up songs of
praise to You, knowing they will bring the fullness of Your
indwelling presence to flood my soul with Your healing light.
In Jesus' name I pray.

COMING *to* FATHER GOD *in* CONFIDENCE

⤎ Read and Consider ⤏
1 John 5:13-21

"This is the confidence we have in approaching God: that if we ask anything according to his will, he hears us. And if we know that he hears us—whatever we ask—we know that we have what we asked of him" (1 John 5:14-15).

The Bible says our relationship to God is like a child's relationship with an adoring father. John spoke of God lavishing His love on us, calling us His own. What a powerful picture of the way we should always approach our heavenly Father. Imagine a small child coming to ask his or her father for something, knowing that it will be given. Would there be any hesitation before the child leaped into the father's arms, relaxed in the safety and security found there? Wouldn't the child be expectant and hopeful as every need is communicated and met?

How does that compare with the way we approach God? Too often we don't bound into His presence as joyfully as a small child. Perhaps we are worried that we're bothering Him with the same old request we've been praying about for years. Or maybe we fear that He is going to deny our request, and we don't want to set ourselves up for disappointment. Or perhaps we feel less than fit to be in His presence because of an area where we feel we are failing.

Whatever the reason we hesitate to come before God with confidence, we know from these verses that He is a good God who hears our requests and cares about our needs. If what we are asking for is wrong for us, He'll let us know. If it's right, He'll make it happen in His way and in His time. We can trust Him enough to run into His presence like a child who is loved and accepted, who can't imagine receiving anything but goodness from Father God.

Heavenly Father, it gives me great confidence to know
that if I ask according to Your will, You will hear
my prayers and answer them. I come to You as Your
beloved child and ask You to teach me how to pray
according to Your will. I know I will receive only good
things from You because You love and accept me. Help
me to understand what Your will is at all times.
In Jesus' name I pray.

Other Books by
Stormie Omartian

The Power of a Praying® Woman
In *The Power of a Praying® Woman*, you'll find personal illustrations, carefully selected Scriptures, and heartfelt prayers to help you trust God with deep longings, cover every area of your life with prayer, and maintain a right heart before Him.

Lead Me, Holy Spirit
Stormie has written books on prayer that have helped millions of people talk to God. Now she focuses on the Holy Spirit and how He wants you to listen to His gentle leading when He speaks to your heart, soul, and spirit. He wants to help you enter into the relationship with God you yearn for and the wholeness and freedom He has for you. He wants to lead you into a better life than you could ever possibly live without Him.

Prayer Warrior
Stormie says, "There is already a war going on around you, and you are in it whether you want to be or not. There is a spiritual war of good and evil—between God and His enemy—and God wants us to stand strong on His side, the side that wins. We win the war when pray in power because prayer *is* the battle." This book will help you become a powerful prayer warrior who understands the path to victory.

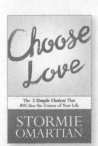

Choose Love
We reflect God most clearly when we are motivated by the power of love in all we say and do. But first we have to understand the depth of God's love for us and receive it. Then we must learn how to effectively express our love for Him.

To learn more about Harvest House books and
to read sample chapters, visit our website:

www.harvesthousepublishers.com

HARVEST HOUSE PUBLISHERS
EUGENE, OREGON